Glenn v. Hobby
8-1-03

Leo Mazzone's Tales from the Braves Mound

Leo Mazzone
With Scott Freeman

SPORTS PUBLISHING L.L.C.
WWW.SPORTSPUBLISHINGLLC.COM

Developmental editor: Gabe A. Rosen
Senior project manager: Jennifer L. Polson
Dust jacket designer: Christine F. Mohrbacher
Copy editor: Cynthia L. McNew

Photos throughout the interior courtesy of Leo Mazzone.

Portions of this book appeared in *Atlanta Magazine.*

ISBN: 1-58261-674-4

Printed in the United States.

SPORTS PUBLISHING L.L.C.
www.sportspublishingllc.com

For Johnny Sain

CONTENTS

PREFACE

By Scott Freeman

Almost every night it was the same: the old man and the kid, crowded into the old man's tiny motor home near the Atlanta Braves' spring training complex in West Palm Beach, Florida, drinking toddies and talking baseball into the wee hours. Well, not exactly talking. The kid was smart enough to do most of the listening. Sometimes the old man would talk about his playing days, like the time he went up against Bob Feller in the opener of the '48 World Series and beat him 1-0. Then there was the time he threw the first pitch that Jackie Robinson ever faced in the major leagues. And he also was on the mound when Babe Ruth came to bat for the very last time in a formal game.

The kid had grown up idolizing Whitey Ford. Well, the old man had plenty of stories about him. Whitey won 25 games one season under his tutelage. And there was the time in 1968 that he coached Denny McLain to a 31-win season. And how about his other star pitcher in Detroit, portly Mickey Lolich, who won three games in the '68 World Series, the last against the legendary Bob Gibson and the Cardinals on just two days' rest? The stories were endless. And the old man told them in a sweet, awe-struck voice that left no doubt that he'd enjoyed every second of his career. Even after all his years in the game, all the ups and downs, he'd never grown cynical about baseball.

Most of all, the old man talked about pitching. Pitching was his first and lasting love. He'd talk about mechanics, how certain pitches worked. Then the importance of changing speeds, even changing deliveries.

"A pitch is made up of several things—velocity, movement, change of speeds, motion," the old man would say. "I have an article where Cy Young was talking about seeing me pitch. And he said when he came up, he had a good overhand fastball and a good overhand curve. He thought that was enough, until he started pitching against Ty Cobb and Cap Anson and people like that. So he started changing his motion, and he noticed I would do that, too—throw a pitch three-quarters or sidearm. I had to do that, because I didn't have an overpowering fastball."

The old man also talked about the mental side: how a coach has to deal with a pitcher's psyche, be a teacher and not a dictator. His most steadfast conviction—that pitchers ought to throw off the mound as often as possible—flew right in the face of conventional baseball wisdom. Starting pitchers were taught to virtually avoid the mound between starts, to let their arms rest.

The old man thought that was all wrong. "How does a runner build endurance?" he'd ask the kid. "He runs. How can a pitcher build endurance if he doesn't throw? You can learn a lot about your pitches by throwing at half-speed or three-quarters— the feel, the spin, the motion. Throwing in the bullpen, you're learning all the time."

The old man went to nine World Series as a player or coach. He'd won at least 20 games in four different seasons, relying on his wits more than his fastball. And he'd also coached more 20-game winners than anyone else in the history of baseball. He was a genuine pitching guru. And he'd always hoped to find someone he could teach, someone who would master his philosophies and then carry them forward.

Johnny Sain had finally found him. Leo Mazzone became his Chosen Disciple.

More than 20 years later, Mazzone has become the Johnny Sain of his generation, the best pitching coach in the business. The numbers don't lie. During one stretch in the '90s, he had coached five out of the last six Cy Young Award winners from the National League. His staff routinely leads the majors in earned run average. Two of his aces, Greg Maddux and Tom Glavine, are headed to Cooperstown; a third, John Smoltz, also could make it.

Of course, the much-heralded pitching staff is the cornerstone of the Braves' dynasty. Leo contends that they are the greatest starting staff ever assembled, and it's difficult to argue with the proposition. There may have been better pitching staffs overall, but none who were so excellent for so long.

It seems impossible that it has been 12 years, over a *decade*, since the Miracle Season of 1991.

It's easy to forget that the Braves were once the laughingstocks of baseball. They lost 106 games in 1988. Then 97 games in both 1989 and 1990. They had finished dead last in four of the last five seasons. The losing seemed destined to go on forever. Which is why 1991 was so stunning, so magical, so unforgettable. Worst to first. Who could have known it was the beginning of a decade-long reign as the most dominant team in the National League?

In 2001, the three pitchers and Leo Mazzone gathered for a portrait to commemorate the extraordinary run of excellence. Appropriately enough, the photograph, by Charlie McCullers, was taken in the old Atlanta-Fulton County Stadium dugout that now resides in the Braves Museum at Turner Field.

None of the players had ever visited the museum, and they spent 10 or 15 minutes exploring the exhibits. Maddux stopped in front of a framed poster that contains baseball cards from past Braves All-Stars. "Hmmm, I wonder how many of these guys I faced," he mused aloud. Maddux studied a row of cards from the '80s. He lifted a finger and pointed to a picture of third baseman Bob Horner. "Didn't face him," Maddux said. His finger then went down the row. "Faced him, didn't face him, faced him, had to hit him once, faced him, faced him."

The player he'd thrown at was Pascual Perez, the gifted but eccentric pitcher who epitomized the old Braves: Perez once missed a start because he spent two hours circling Atlanta on I-285 on the theory it would eventually lead him to the Stadium. Maddux was asked why he threw at Perez. "Ah, you know," he shrugged, "it was just one of those things."

Finally, Smoltz called the others down to the end of the room. "Hey, you've got to see this," he said. And there they were, perhaps the greatest starting pitching staff in the history of the game, quietly crowded around an old Atlanta Stadium locker that contained memorabilia from the 1991 season. For a moment, they were nothing more than baseball fans. Standing in awe just like any fan would.

There is a striking bond between Leo and his pitchers. Sometimes he's a benevolent teacher. Sometimes the encouraging father. Other times the screaming drill sergeant. But they all know he cares. Deeply. When they win, he steers the praise to them; when they fail, he deflects the criticisms aimed at them. He has but one goal: to see his pitchers succeed. "He's never been a self-promoter, almost to the point he's about as invisible as anybody could be with that pitching staff," Fox Sports baseball analyst Tim McCarver told me once. "It wouldn't be that unusual for a pitching coach to take credit for those guys. But Leo seems content to stay in the background. And that makes him more appealing. Because he's really legitimate. He's smart as a whip. He's about as honest a guy as you'll meet—no BS. And he has almost revolutionized the way you handle pitchers."

The old man is long retired now, and he visibly brightens whenever he talks about the kid. They stay in contact. Ever so often, he'll pack up some of the memorabilia from his career and he'll ship it off to the kid's home for safekeeping.

Long ago he gave a gift of even greater importance—all the wisdom he had accumulated through 27 years of major-league baseball. His trust has been affirmed. Johnny Sain's legacy lives through the kid who dared to listen.

FOREWORD

By John Smoltz

I came to Atlanta from a different organization with very different philosophies. I'd just undergone this whole transformation in Detroit where they changed all of my mechanics and my pitches. I had a pretty darned good curveball when I signed with the Detroit Tigers. When I got there, they said it was too big and that I'd never be able to control it. I was a confused young pitcher, and Leo really helped me get on track. When I got to Atlanta in 1987, he told me, "You've got a great delivery. Now let's just work on upgrading your pitches."

It's probably not the most profound thing to say, but for me it was the best thing I could possibly have heard. And the best timing. I thought I was pretty good, but my career was in chaos. With Leo, I could relax and not worry about everything else. And that was a big turnaround for me.

Leo showed me the throw-turn-and-pull curveball. I was able to pick it up pretty quick, and over time, I was able to master it. In fact, I made it through the first part of my career on just two pitches—that curveball and the fastball.

In tutoring young pitchers and trying to mentor them into the big leagues, he stayed on us pretty hard. To the point of challenging certain guys, hoping deep down that they would never accept his challenge. Just seeing how animated he could get at times was always fun to watch.

Say what you will, the one thing he gave you was the sense that he would fight for you. If he believed in you, he was going to fight for you. He's put a lot of work into what he believes. And when someone's teaching you, you've got to know they believe in what they're teaching.

When I got called up to Atlanta, they sent him to Shea Stadium to watch my major-league debut. It was neat to have him there. Gosh, I was scared to death. Knowing what we'd been through together that year and what he had put me through, it was nice to know that if I needed to look over there, I could. That game went in stages. Parts of it were in slow motion, and parts went by really fast. I'd look over there every so often, and a couple of times I saw him flicking his wrist as if to tell me to throw a curveball.

Leo has stuck with me through some hard times, like when I was struggling pretty bad during my 2-11 stretch in 1991. I appreciated how he handled it and how he continued to believe in me. There was one game where the catcher had already been out to get on me. Then Leo came out and got on me, too. I kicked the mound and said, "I'm trying. Look, the catcher's already chewed me out, and now you've chewed me out. I don't need to be double-teamed."

And he said, "Oh, you're right. I'm sorry." Then he went back to the dugout.

One of the funniest moments in my entire life was in Triple A when I was playing for Richmond. We were all young and dumb still. And in every season, you come to a point where you just don't play well or it's just not working real well. Sometimes you need shock treatment. Leo tried to provide it.

We were really struggling on a road trip to Oklahoma. Some bad things happened in this particular game. I remember Leo just racing over to this huge garbage can by the dugout and kicking it as hard as he could. It didn't budge an inch. We all thought he'd broken his foot. So then he tried to dump it over, and he was going to jump on it. Except it didn't move an inch. Turns out it was cemented to the floor.

We've laughed a lot; we've been through a lot. It's not like I'm a pitcher who came in and took everybody by storm. It's not like I'm a pitcher who's had good health all my life. With the exception of a couple of doctors and trainers, he's the only one who really understands what I've gone through in my career. He's in that line, one of the very few people. You're in war together.

I've literally only had a couple of pitching coaches in my life. Of all the pitchers, I've been with Leo the longest. More than Glavine, more than anybody. When you spend that much time together, you build up a relationship. I mean, he's been my pitching coach for just about my entire career.

We used to go at one another all the time when the Boston Celtics and Detroit Pistons were dueling in the playoffs. He was always on top. Finally, I got him. For two straight years, the Pistons won it all. Now it's our Michigan State-Notre Dame battles. Which, until last year, I had the upper hand. I don't worry.

There's always next year.

PREGAME

My phone rang in the 2002 off season, just before Christmas. Tommy Glavine was a free agent and had just signed with the New York Mets; now, everybody was speculating about whether Greg Maddux would also go with another team. Our one and two starters. Both future Hall of Famers. Gone. I didn't want to think about it. I picked up the phone. "Hey Coach."

"Yeah?"

"This is player." It was Maddux.

We chatted a while before I popped the question: "What are you gonna do, Mad Dog?"

"Well, I'm just hoping we can do *something*," he said.

He kept his house in Atlanta; that was a hint right there. But you really don't get a read on Maddux like that because of his ability to play a poker face. The Braves offered him arbitration, but there was absolutely nothing in the press from him or his agents. So I'm sitting there waiting on a bomb to drop,

MAZZONE WATCHING MADDUX WARM UP IN THE BRAVES BULLPEN.

and then he accepts arbitration and says, "This is the place I wanted to stay all along." That's typical Mad Dog. Not just a great pitcher, a great person. He knows the right way to do things. He knows the right way to go about your business professionally.

There was a game he pitched in New York against the Mets, and he got knocked out in the second inning. Most runs he'd ever given up in an inning and two-thirds. It's just a game where he got down the middle. The only time he's going to give up runs is if he ends up missing on some pitches down the middle. So he came off the field with the crowd all over him.

His next start was at Turner Field against the Mets. After six or seven innings, he had a shutout going. Seventy-one pitches. And he came in and said, "I'm done."

"Are you kidding?" I said. "You're doing great out there."

"No," he said. "I am *done*."

So we made the move to the bullpen and we won. After the game, he came up and said, "You had a surprised look on your face when I told you I was done. You didn't think I was, did you?"

"My God, you're throwing a shutout, you don't have many pitches, I thought you looked great," I said. "You didn't show any signs of being physically tired to me."

And he said, "I'm going to tell you why I was done, Leo. With the standards that are set for me, and the standards that are set for myself, nobody can understand what it's like walking off the mound after getting your ass kicked. I got embarrassed in New York. From the moment I started to walk off that field, I was preparing for my next start against that team. I knew my next start was against them and I was going to make darned sure that it didn't happen again. The reason I told you I was tired wasn't because I was physically tired; it was because I put so much thought process into it. I was mentally shot. It's all I thought of for four days and nobody can understand my feelings coming off that mound that day in New York but me."

Mad Dog commands a tremendous amount of respect from the people within the game. It's no accident. He is that intelligent. He prepares. That's well known around the baseball circles. We were at Yankee Stadium during interleague play. Mad Dog was pitching a tremendous game. And John Hirschbeck was umpiring behind the plate. Maddux was coming off the mound in the third inning, and I saw Hirschbeck walk over to him and say something. When he got to the dugout, I said, "Mad Dog, what's the umpire telling you?"

"He told me that I was as good as advertised," Maddux said. "Isn't that great? Now I not only have to please Bobby and you and the Braves, *and* live up to my reputation with the Yankees, now I've got to deal with pressure from the umpire that I'm that good."

Another time, he had the bases loaded in Philadelphia, two out. Jerry Crawford was the second base umpire and he was set up behind the mound. I saw Maddux turn around and talk to Crawford, nod his head, come back, throw a pitch, strike the guy out. He came in and I asked what he and Crawford were talking about. He said, "Well, I just went back off the mound and told Jerry, 'I don't know whether to throw this guy a fastball or a change-up. What do you think?' He said he thought he'd throw a change-up. So I threw him a change-up and struck him out."

It was very close to Christmas when I found out that Mad Dog was coming back for the 2003 season. Bobby Cox had called a few days earlier and said he felt Maddux might stay with us. I waited on pins and needles like everybody else.

I was out Christmas shopping and somebody came up and said, "Don't worry, he signed." I got back and it was on ESPN, and I went, "All right!"

I had it backwards. I always thought that Mad Dog would leave and Glavine would stay. It's too bad that both of them couldn't finish their careers in a Braves uniform, then go into the Hall of Fame together. There's a lot of sentiment in that. They used to call them "The Young Guns." It doesn't happen in baseball all that often, where you have great pitchers like Glavine and Maddux and John Smoltz on one staff who all have a good chance of going into the Hall of Fame. They all could be going in with the same uniform on. That still might happen. I can't visualize Tommy Glavine in a Mets uniform in the Hall of Fame.

I didn't talk to Tommy before he made his decision. He called after he signed with the Mets. He said there were certain things … that it was just a decision he had to make. He didn't have a whole lot to say. We thanked each other, personally, for everything over the years. I told him, "When you pitch against us, I hope you pitch well and get a no-decision … and we win."

With Tommy, I look at that more from the personal point of view than the professional—the times spent together and the pressures of all the pennant races. It's like Maddux and Glavine told me, they've never pitched a game in Atlanta when their team didn't have a chance for the pennant, 12 years in a row. And then all the postseasons we've had. I think you're describing something that's unique, where there might be a few more personal feelings felt than normal.

We traded Kevin Millwood in the off season. He wasn't with us for long, but he fits into that category, too. A first-class guy. Like Steve Avery, who was one of the original Young Guns. When I saw Steve pitching for Boston a couple of years back, it made me sick. You can't help but get personally attached to them over a period of time. Very attached. These guys have been here a long time and had a tremendous amount of success. Maddux for 10 years, Tommy for 12, Smoltzie for 12. Sure, there are a lot of emotional ties involved.

Those pitchers have put my name on the map. I sure as hell didn't do it. It was their performance. And TBS. It's hard to see Glavine and Millwood go, because you're talking 400 innings a year. Good innings, too. I'll tell you what, Millwood was as good as anybody on our staff last year. So, yeah, I hate to see him go. He'll be very difficult against us when we go to Philly. There's a big mound in Philadelphia and he's a big man.

The front office has to combine the personal and the professional. John Schuerholz, the Braves' general manager, always emphasizes that you have to manage change effectively. And I don't think anybody has done that better than the Braves. Of course, your mainstays have always been there. Some of them are gone now. But we still have Maddux and we still have Smoltzie. And now we have Ray Ortiz, who's one of the better pitchers in the National League. We have Mike Hampton, who was one of the best pitchers in the National League and will be again. We have Paul Byrd, who rejuvenated his career in Kansas City. And Jason Marquis, who can come along at any time. It ends up a strong rotation. You've just got to have that big dog at the top, and that's Maddux.

Like Bobby Cox says, you can never have enough pitching.

OPENING PITCH:
WHERE DREAMS ARE BORN

My career with the Braves began in 1979. I had retired as a player, never made the big leagues. I was signed in 1967 as a left-handed pitcher out of high school by the San Francisco Giants. My first professional experience was in Medford, Oregon. We had workouts there for 10 or 12 days. Then we played each other to determine who went to the rookie league in Salt Lake City and who would stay with the Class A team in Medford.

They told me I was pitching the fourth and fifth inning of the second game. I went out there and struck out the side. I was five foot nine, 160 pounds. They said, "Hey, for a little guy you throw good."

I just told them right to their face: "See all those big guys over there? I throw better than them, too." I didn't have to go to the rookie league. I made the Class A team when I was 17 years old.

Baseball was always my sport. My dad worked in a paper mill 45 years. He'd get off work and catch me every night at the park. And we'd work on pitching. When I was growing up, we had cement blocks under our porch. I used to color the corners of the cement blocks with pieces of coal. And then try to hit those corners. I pitched a long time in my life without walking too many guys, and that's what I credit it to. And I'd go out and mimic the deliveries of the great pitchers like Whitey Ford and Warren Spahn.

There was never a day that went by when I didn't go to the ballpark. I didn't have to have somebody with me. I'd grab a bat and a ball, and I'd go down there and find someone. If it rained, it'd make me sick. Especially if it was the day I was scheduled to pitch. I think that's when I probably said my first curse words. I'd look up and say, "Oh, no, we're going to get rained out." And I'd looked so forward to this ballgame, putting my "uni" on and knowing I was going to go out and pitch. I can still remember that feeling to this day. The feeling of going out and pitching, and the feeling of being disappointed if we had bad weather. And in western Maryland where I grew up, it wasn't automatic you were going to have sunshine.

Why did I take to baseball? When you say "the big leagues," it has a magic to it. It's a part of your growing up. Listening to those games on the radio was awesome. You'd sit there and listen to them on your little transistor. You couldn't wait to get out of school to listen. And if a station wouldn't come in, then you were cussing again. I'd be glued to the *Game of the Week* on television, Pee Wee Reese and Dizzy Dean. I'd listen to Mel Allen with the Yankees and Bob Prince with the Pirates. Chuck Thompson with the Orioles. Everybody identifies with major-league baseball. It's the whole package.

I was signed out of high school by a scout named Chick Genovese for 400 bucks. I said, "Where's my bonus?"

He said, "You're kinda small. You'll make all your money once you reach the big leagues."

About 23 years later, I got to the big leagues. My 23 years in the minor leagues, I enjoyed every minute of it. When I was pitching, I couldn't wait for the season to start. When I was coaching, I couldn't wait for the season to start. I made the starting rotation of the Single-A team in Medford. I went 6-6, pitched 94 innings and struck out 94. I more than held my own out there, and I learned quite a bit. I was very surprised my first year to see beer in the clubhouse, or somebody lighting up a cigarette. We used to call them "dirts." I was very surprised; that's how naive I was. And, of course, some of the tirades from the manager. Back then, they managed by intimidation. You were afraid to say anything to them.

The one year I remember was 1969 in Class A in Decatur, Illinois, when I either set or tied a Midwest League record with 17 complete games. I also had 15 wins that year. In 1972, I was 9-8 and won the ERA crown with a 2.26 ERA in Amarillo in the Texas League. But I fell two or three innings short of qualifying for the official ERA title. I was supposed to start the last day of the season, but my teammates flooded the field because we were out of the pennant race and they didn't want to play. I cussed all of them out as they were leaving the clubhouse. I was really mad.

I had good seasons in the minors; then they made me a reliever. It was the politics of the game. The bigger your signing bonus, the more chances you have to fail.

When you don't sign for any money, you have to keep making a spot for yourself every year, and I did that for a long time. That's a lesson I learned on my way up: the top guys got all the attention, and the other guys got ignored. So I make

LEO MAZZONE ON THE MOUND FOR THE AMARILLO GIANTS.

sure that I don't do that as a coach now, because I know how I felt on the other end of it.

The way I look at it, I didn't get a bonus. To pitch for 10 years and not have a signing bonus, or any money invested in you at all by the organization, that says you're a pretty damned good pitcher. Because nobody's going to let you last that long. I loved every minute of it. After I pitched ten years, Oakland started talking to me about coaching. They said I was coaching or managing material and set me up with my first job managing.

I went down to Corpus Christi, Texas in the Independent League in 1976 to manage, and we won the pennant two years in a row. I thought I was the smartest SOB in the world. The league ran out of money, and I got a call from the Carolina League to manage the co-op team in Kinston. There's where the connection with the Braves started. Every organization in the league would option out three or four players to fill my team's roster. I had to run my own camp 10 days prior to the season because I had to wait for the various teams to send them from spring training to Kinston. We put together a team that pitched great. We finished in fourth place and were at the top of the league in pitching and defense. That's when Paul Snyder, who was the director of scouting for the Braves, and Hank Aaron, who was the director of player development, expressed interest in me. They saw the development of our pitchers, and how well the team performed with lesser talent.

In 1979, the Braves invited me down to Sarasota where they had their instructional league. I met Hank Aaron at the airport in Atlanta and I was a nervous wreck. We got on the plane to fly to Sarasota, and we hit it off right away on the plane. It turned out he was my boss for the next 12 years. I thought they were hiring me to manage. Hank said, "No, we want you to be the pitching coach."

And I said, "Well, I can do both. That's what I've been doing since 1976."

He said, "No, no, you don't understand how this works. We want you to be the pitching coach."

We were watching pitchers down there and he asked me to watch them throw. And I didn't know anybody, didn't have a clue. He said, "Pick out who you think has the best arm." Well, it wasn't that tough to pick out Steve Bedrosian, who went on to win the Cy Young Award.

LESSONS FROM A PITCHING GURU

On that first day of spring training, Hank told me he wanted to introduce me to someone. And he called over Johnny Sain, who was the team's pitching coach at the Triple-A team in Richmond. He took me under his wing; I thought you'd have to be a fool not to pick the brain of the man who had coached the most 20-game winners and the most Cy Young winners and the most World Series pitchers of any pitching coach in the history of baseball. Johnny was the last guy to ever pitch to Babe Ruth in an organized baseball game and the first to pitch to Jackie Robinson in a major-league game. He won 20 games four times. Then he coached nine different pitchers to 20-win seasons, including Whitey Ford, Ralph Terry, Jim Bouton, Mudcat Grant, Jim Kaat and Denny McLain.

It became a very close-knit relationship. In spring training and the instructional leagues, he wouldn't stay in a motel. He had an RV and he would hook it up. So after the workouts, I would go over to his RV and we'd cook, maybe have a little toddy and talk about pitching. And just do it for a couple of hours. You know, he's got a track record. The greatest track record in the history of the game. He was so helpful in my thought process and my approach. He was the smartest son of a gun and the nicest guy I'd ever talked to. He had all these things to offer. Believe it or not, there were some people who wouldn't listen to him. I think sometimes he was so far ahead of his time that those other people feared his knowledge, so, therefore, they turned it off. Whatever their reason was, they were stupid. I went the exact opposite. I was going to jump all over it and listen to everything he had to say.

A lot of the other pitching coaches thought his philosophies would ruin pitchers' arms because he had them throwing all the time. That was a misread. What you have to understand was that he had them throwing all the time without throwing hard. And that's the same thing we've put in place here in Atlanta. It works. If you regulate the effort, you can get on the mound as often as possible and you're not going to know what your pitches do unless you practice them. It's the philosophy of our organization that you get on the mound as often as possible, and it goes back to Johnny Sain.

At that time, we were pretty much on our own within the organization. The reason I loved working for Hank was that he said, "Here's your pitching staff; you take care of them." He gave me free rein to do what I wanted. It was a great way to allow your coaches to work. I used to worry because I wouldn't hear from him for a long time. So I called him up and said, "Hank, is everything all right? I haven't heard from you."

And he said, "Leo, when I don't call, that means everything is fine. Be glad I'm not calling a lot."

Johnny was way ahead of everybody else. He didn't give the usual clichés when it came to what he was teaching me. He taught me everything from throwing programs to proper spins on a baseball to strategies of baseball to dealing with the front office. Everything he talked to me about and taught me, I've seen it all unfold from the top down. It was a tremendous education.

GETTING ESTABLISHED

Once Bobby Cox became the general manager in 1986, that's when things picked up in my personal career. Bobby wanted to turn an offensive-oriented team into a pitching-oriented team. He had a meeting and wanted to know who was going to take care of the pitchers. There were various pitching coaches in the room, and I jumped up. I'd already had a history of pitchers in the minor leagues making all their starts. We never seemed to have pitchers going down. It was something that's worked out everywhere I've been, from A ball to the major leagues. I explained my pitching programs to him: throwing more often with less exertion, throwing twice in between starts. I explained to him the proper way to do it, to develop pitchers.

The general philosophy in baseball then was that pitchers should do one session throwing off the mound in between starts. I wanted to do two. The reason for this is to close the gap between a four- and five-man rotation. The baseball world has now gone to a five-man rotation for health reasons. I've always felt you stayed sharper in four. So I wanted to combine that, so they would stay as sharp as though they were in a four,

MAZZONE AND BOBBY COX ON "THROWBACK UNIFORM" DAY.

yet healthy in a five. I did it on my own in the minor leagues and it worked.

There was one coach in particular who said that if we had pitchers throw that much, their arms would be dead in August. So I asked him what he did. He said he had them play catch out in the outfield. I asked him to explain the difference between pitchers playing catch in the outfield and being on the mound with a catcher squatted down behind home plate and playing catch that way. He said they would have the tendency to throw too hard. My answer was: that's what they pay you for, to regulate the effort. And then Bobby said, "Leo's programs are in place."

Regulating the effort is the key. All the pitchers I've come into contact with love the program. There are a lot of coaches who either don't want to do it or don't believe in it. Or else they can't regulate the effort and can't organize it. But I don't really care what other coaches want to do. I know the proper way to do it over the long haul. And it's worked. If you've noticed in the last 12 years, our strength has been in August and September. And into October. I'm very proud of our health record over that time and the innings pitched. The guys not missing starts and taking pride in not missing starts.

When Bobby became the general manager of the Braves, Atlanta-Fulton County Stadium was known as "The Launching Pad." It was considered death to pitchers. It used to be that the Braves would score a lot of runs and always be near the bottom in staff ERA. Bobby worked closely with me in the minor leagues. I'd be on the phone with him a lot, telling him about the projected rotation for the future. He told me, "If somebody moves up, you might not necessarily follow them up the chain. Just go where I tell you." That was fine with me.

In 1987, we traded Doyle Alexander to the Detroit Tigers for a minor-league pitcher named John Smoltz. Bobby called me to tell me about the trade. He said, "Take John down to Sarasota. He's got a great fastball. Doesn't have another pitch. I don't know about his delivery. He was 4-10 in double A, but he has a great arm."

I had a one-on-one with John down in the Instructional League after the trade, and it worked out extremely well. What I did with him sounds so simple. And it was. He was throwing a little bit and I said, "John, I want you to do one thing for me."

He said, "What's that, Leo?"

I said, "I want you to throw the most natural way you want to throw." He wound up and threw the pitch, and I told him, "That is absolutely great."

He turned around and said, "What do you mean? What am I doing wrong?"

I said, "You're not doing anything wrong."

He said, "Well, in Detroit they tried to get me to do this and do that."

"Look," I said. "Do it again."

He was able to do it again and he said, "Is that all there is to it?"

"Yeah," I said. "You have so much coordination, just let your natural athleticism come out."

It was one of the most beautiful deliveries I'd ever seen. And then I taught him a breaking ball, the Johnny Sain throw-turn-and-pull breaking ball. It was a breaking ball that Sain taught me that he also had taught to Whitey Ford and Ralph Terry and Mudcat Grant and Mickey Lolich and Denny McClain and Jim Kaat and the list goes on and on. It's a breaking ball that's centered in your hand. And your thought process is to throw it before you turn it. A lot of guys want to turn it early. Johnny always wanted you to throw it first because you had a more powerful position with it and you could take the strain off your elbow. There were three steps to it. You want to throw the ball, then spin it, then turn your arm in.

Smoltzie was able to get that real quick. He threw a couple of them and they broke pretty good. He threw a couple of more and they broke real good. And I'm sitting there thinking I couldn't be this smart. But he was able to throw the best curveball that I've ever seen from a right-handed pitcher.

I called Bobby up and told him John was doing fine, that he had a beautiful delivery and a great fastball and good breaking stuff and that his control was good.

He said, "Are you crazy?" The next year, Jim Beauchamp and I were put together in Richmond as manager and pitching coach. We talked Bobby into letting us take Smoltz with us to Richmond. And by July he was in the big leagues.

It's funny. Johnny Sain told me one time you can hurt more guys by over-coaching than you can the other way around. All I did with John was allow him to be himself. And he had a beautiful delivery. Taught him a breaking ball, and he was off from there. John's style was a fly ball, strikeout pitcher. Some people were concerned about that at the Launching Pad. But you can't let a ballpark dictate the style that you're going to pitch. You have to let the individual do that.

For example, when Steve Avery signed I had him in the minor leagues. I didn't teach Steve Avery a pitch. He had them. So my job was to see that he kept them. And that worked out real well, too.

AVERY HAD A KILLER MENTALITY ON THE MOUND.

Smoltzie in the early part of his career got a little anxious and impatient. But he was able to settle in and become a great pitcher. Avery had the killer instinct that was well above a lot of people. And Tommy Glavine, I only had him for a short time in the Instructional League. That cool demeanor and the stoic figure, he had that when he was young. Smoltzie had to develop to get a little bit more control of his emotions. Tommy had his emotions in check. And Avery was a killer.

They all went through difficult times before having success, every single one of them. You have to remind yourself of that all the time so that you don't run out of patience with a pitcher who is having a little trouble when he's out there pitching. When you run out of patience with a pitcher is when they don't prepare, don't dedicate themselves.

We knew we were building the nucleus of a great pitching staff. The names that always came up were John Smoltz, Steve Avery, Tommy Greene, Pete Smith, Kent Mercker, Mike Stanton. Glavine had already made the big leagues. That's a long list there. I always remind people, in '91 there were some young kids who took us to the seventh game of the World Series. In '92, we threw 24 shutouts. And that was the year before Maddux got to Atlanta. Bobby could have traded those guys when he was still the general manager for a quick fix to get his team up to .500. But with the pitching prospects in the organization and how it was coming together, he was going to ride it out. He had the patience to stay with it.

I got called up to the big leagues from Richmond in 1990. We'd just finished a game on the road; Derek Lilliquist had thrown a shutout. And Bobby called me up in the lobby of a hotel. He said, "Can you be in Atlanta tomorrow?"

I said, "Yeah, what's going on?"

He said, "I don't want you to go crazy, I know how excitable you can be. You're going to be the pitching coach of the Atlanta Braves. It's time to take these guys and go." So I just sat there in silence. And he said, "Well, don't you have anything to say?"

I said, "Yeah, I just have one question: who's the manager?"

And he said, "Me."

I smiled, and I said, "I'll be right there."

ATLANTA RISING

After all those years in baseball, 23, to be named pitching coach of the Braves and for Bobby Cox to be the manager was the best situation that I could possibly have had. And 12 years later, I'm still here. It's the realization of all my boyhood dreams.

The secret of the Braves is that Bobby got the pitching going when he was general manager. Then when John Schuerholz became the general manager, he was able to acquire a great defense in a short period of time. The two go hand in hand. I remember we had great young starters when I came to Atlanta in June of 1990.

Our starters were pitching well, but it was going unnoticed because the Braves were in last place. Glav had a good September, Smoltzie was getting his stuff together, Av was starting to grow a little bit, and Pete Smith was doing well.

We got to Atlanta, and it was an easy transition because I'd had a lot of the pitchers in the minor leagues. I gave them my programs and got them organized. You can't get anything done if you're not prepared and organized—being in the bullpen at the proper time, doing your physicals at the proper time, preparing for the opposition at the proper time, getting your time schedule down to where there's no dead time or as little as possible. Always talking about pitching.

We got there and Bobby told me, "Look, I don't care if you don't pick up a ball during batting practice; you go take care of those pitchers." He was right. You learn a lot just by being with them. You have to be with them, whether they're on the mound or wherever they're at. Talking to them all the time. Making sure that if you have 11 people on your staff, that number 11 is getting the same amount of attention as number one.

That's part of the throwing program, actually. Have your starters come up, then your relievers. Explain to them how you want to do it. Develop a relationship with all of them. There was a five-something staff ERA going on. So I said, "Look, let's have a goal from this day to the end of the season; let's get the staff ERA down under four." It was too late to do it; there were too many innings accumulated to get it down that far. But you had to give them a goal of some sort because we weren't going to win anything as far as the standings. We almost did it. From the day Bobby and I started until the end of the season, we had a 4.02 staff ERA.

Glav was 10-12 that year. But I think he won four in September. That was really the first time I'd spent a lot of time with him. What immediately impressed me was his work ethic, the consistency of his work ethic. His routines never changed once we defined them. He took it from there and loved it. He developed a sequence of how he wanted to prepare, and I didn't see it change in 12 years. He never strayed from it, regardless of the outcome of the game he'd just pitched. If there is one pitcher who defines the throwing programs that we believe in, Tommy would be the leader of the pack. He got to the point that if he didn't throw, he didn't feel right. That's what you want. You want them to the point of where if they don't throw, they don't feel right. Because if you don't throw, it's not going to work because you're never going to be able to improve your pitches.

Steve Avery was 3-11 and having a difficult time. Here's an example of why Bobby Cox is the best pitcher's manager in baseball. Avery got beat up pretty good in a ballgame, and so he was upset and went into clubhouse. Bobby said to me, "Listen, we'll take care of things out here; why don't you go inside and be with Av."

He was sitting in his locker, staring at it. And I walked in and just sat with him. I said, "So you're upset."

"Yeah."

"You let everybody down."

"Yeah."

"You let yourself down, you let your parents down."

"Yeah."

"You're letting the Braves down."

"Yeah."

"Just remember one thing. Once you get acclimated to your environment, payback's gonna be a bitch for the rest of the National League."

Just being there and sitting there with him probably helped more than going out to the bullpen to work on mechanics. I'll tell you what, he was a killer.

Bobby did a great thing at the end of 1990. He told me to bring Glavine, Smoltz, Avery, Pete Smith and Charlie Leibrandt out to the dugout. Bring them out early. And he told them, "You guys be prepared to be the starting rotation in '91. Come to spring training, prepare to get ready for the long haul. You guys are starting every fourth or fifth game in '91."

They did, and they took us all the way to the seventh game of the World Series.

FIRST INNING:
WORST TO FIRST

The Young Guns had matured in 1990, but it went unnoticed. The difference when we got to 1991 was the defense. John Schuerholz became the general manager and he brought in defense. We had a new third baseman, a new shortstop, a new second baseman, a new first baseman, a new center fielder and a new catcher. And they basically were all great defensive players. Terry Pendleton. Rafael Belliard. Sid Bream, Lemmer [Mark Lemke]. You had Otis Nixon in center and David Justice in right.

Bobby had wanted to upgrade the pitching, and everybody knew there were some great arms coming. Then you add defense to it, and there's your mindset. You can't have one without the other. So between Bobby and Schuerholz in '91, we developed a new mindset. And that became a way of destroying the myth of the Launching Pad. They brought in a new grounds crew, and all of a sudden the field became beautiful.

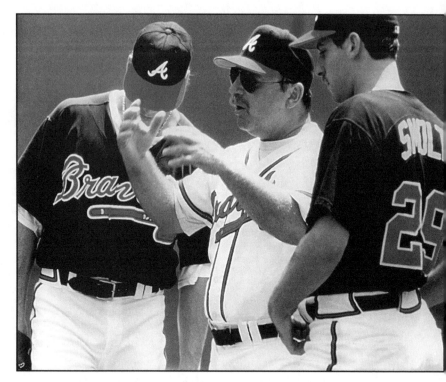

GLAVINE, LEFT, AND SMOLTZ WERE THE TWO KEY MEMBERS OF THE FABLED YOUNG GUNS IN 1991.

Bobby had the kind of patience that allowed the pitching staff to get through some rough times. It wasn't easy. We lost some in the first half, and at the All-Star break we were nine and a half games out. It was an especially rough stretch for Smoltzie. He was 2-11 at the break. It was tough and he was frustrated. Some of it was circumstance; some of it he brought on himself by worrying too much and not being able to get hold of all of his emotions.

When he was 2-11, it didn't seem like he was pitching that badly. You were still going, wow, man, that was a great pitch! It was just a mistake coming at the wrong time, some-thing going a little haywire. He began to understand that some of those things were out of his control. He began to under-stand that he had to just concentrate on what he was going to throw and then execute the pitch. That's when he started not to have as much anxiety.

I tried to be very supportive during that time. Hollering at him and raising Cain was not the right way to go. He was already emotionally tense and a little unsure, wanting so badly to do well. Bobby and I thought he was still throwing the ball extremely well. We tried to point out to him that, hey, you're not as bad as that record sounds; actually, you look pretty good.

There was no question about his stuff; it was a matter of a mistake at the wrong time. Guys you thought he would domi-nate were the ones getting the hits. And guys you thought would hit him, they didn't get hits. If you ask Smoltzie today about the toughest hitters he's ever faced, I don't think he's going to tell you it was Barry Bonds or any of those guys. He's going to tell you it was guys like Brett Butler, the pesky guys. The little fleas, as Earl Weaver used to say. Those were the ones that hit him, the eighth-place hitters. The big guns, he'd smoke them.

By the All-Star break, a lot of people were talking about getting Smoltz out of the starting rotation. As a coach, you stick to what you believe in and let the other stuff go in one ear and out the other. I thought it was a no-brainer that he stay in the rotation. The number-one reason why John Smoltz was able to turn it around in the second half of '91 is that his manager did not take him out of the starting rotation. When Bobby asked me, I told him, "I wouldn't even think about it.

He's got to start. He's a starting pitcher and he's the best 2-11 pitcher I've ever seen." Then Smoltzie got going a little bit. You can't have any confidence unless you have some success. He started rolling, and then he really took off.

Of course, Smoltzie went 12-2 the second half and wound up 14-13 for the season. Avery won 18. Tommy was 20-11 and the Cy Young Award winner. Charlie Leibrandt was supposedly done, and he won 15 ballgames. Charlie was kind of the father figure because he showed Avery, Glavine and Smoltz that you didn't have to throw hard to win, you had to *pitch* to win. Bobby and I would be sitting in the dugout and Charlie's first pitch would be a fastball down and away for a strike. And it was about 80 miles per hour. Bobby would look at me and say, "Well, Leo, there goes the blazer."

And then Charlie would change speeds. When Charlie would change speeds and throw a change-up, it looked like he threw the pitch and then the ball stopped; the batter would swing and then the ball continued on its way.

Charlie was a real class act who was a tremendous help to Avery, Glavine, Smoltz and Pete Smith. He more than held his own. Charlie was in the four-hole, and he won 15 games in '91 and 15 games in '92. That's not too shabby. There are not many teams that could say the four-hole was a 15-game winner.

We caught fire after the All-Star break. We were trying to regain some respectability. It just kept building all year. We had a three-game series in New York in early September. We swept the Mets. That's the first time the Braves had done that in New York in a long time. We pitched Mercker, Leibrandt and Glavine. They all won. We came home to play San Francisco. Smoltz pitched and won; then Avery pitched and won. I remember Bobby looked at me and said, "Leo, I think your young guys are growing up."

DOWN TO THE WIRE

The emotions of the pennant race took over, and that was probably the greatest season I've ever experienced. The atmosphere was unbelievable. When Bobby said that to me, I said to myself, we got something going on here. The young pitchers were starting to pitch like veterans, and you could see it start to gradually develop. Once they finally started to believe, *yeah, we do really belong here*, they took it and ran with it.

We swept St. Louis and then the Dodgers got swept. You look up and you're right there. Now there's a buzz and there's an electricity, now you know you're in it. A pennant race is so much fun. There's no pressure at all. There's fun, there's excitement, there's enjoyment. When you're *not* in a pennant race, or you're not winning ballgames, that's where the pressure is. I feel the most pressure in a season in April and May. You're coming out of the gate and trying to put yourself in the position to be in the pennant race.

Kent Mercker pitched a no-hitter with Mark Wohlers and Alejandro Pena in September. He was spot-starting then and he was done after six innings. We give our pitchers leeway and let them have some input into the process of when they come out of a game, which separates us from a lot of teams. Sometimes it's a difficult decision to take out a pitcher; by the same token, you don't want to hurt anybody. Merck was tired and he was a high pitch-count guy anyway. It was funny, at the end of the game Alejandro didn't even know there was a no-hitter. He threw the ball up in the stands after the game. Couldn't understand why everyone was jumping around.

Alejandro Pena was one of the best relievers we ever had, for the simple fact that he closed games very quietly. Every relief pitcher I come into contact with, I tell them what Alejandro used to tell me. Somebody asked him how he was saving so many games for the Braves. And he said, "Well, because I'm pitching the ninth inning rather than the sixth or seventh." He didn't know what the big deal was. He said, "I've only got to get three outs. I can do that with my fastball."

If more relievers took that approach, I think there'd be a lot less crazy stuff going on in the ninth inning. Every relief pitcher I meet, I tell that story. That was one of the greatest trades we ever made. We picked him up for a left-handed pitcher named Tony Castillo. You might not hear a lot about it, but that was a tremendous trade.

We were thick in the pennant race and enjoying every minute of it. The Dodgers series in late September is still the biggest thrill I've ever had. I remember having to get to the park early because you couldn't get down Capital Avenue past a certain hour. I always got there early anyway, but this was getting there at noon. The weather was beautiful, the ballpark was packed, and the crowds were fantastic. The tomahawk chop was happening, and the noise was just unbelievable. Smoltzie told me that when he was out there pitching, he couldn't believe how loud it was. He said it sounded like the Boston Garden with the Lakers-Celtics. Only you're talking about 60,000 people rather than 13,909.

From that point on, we were running out a starting pitcher who was real good every game. I remember Tommy Lasorda saying, "Yeah, the Braves have a good team; I just wish they'd get off our tail." We lost the first game, and then won the next two. Avery pitched a six-hit shutout. That's why he's the Dodger killer. He was tremendous. You talk about being on the attack. I don't just mean firing heat. I mean on the attack with his fastball and with his change-up. And on the attack with his breaking ball. In other words, attacking with his full assortment, not just trying to rare back and fire.

In Steve's case, he became a great pitcher at an early age because he trusted himself with a change of speeds. He was a power pitcher out of high school and had always been a strikeout pitcher. There are a lot of times when it's going to take a pitcher a long time to trust an off-speed pitch because he's had so much success with his power. Also he might throw one real hard, then throw a change-up and somebody hits it out. And then somebody says, "How in the hell could you throw him that pitch?" I was always one to encourage Steve to change speeds. Guess who taught me that? Maybe a guy named Johnny Sain.

I ran into a Hall of Famer named Eddie Mathews when I was in Triple A; he was a roving hitting instructor. He said, "Leo, tell your pitchers one thing for me. Tell them you can time a jet coming through that strike zone if you see it often enough." I've never forgotten that.

So we were always encouraging Steve not to forget his off-speed pitches. A lot of pitchers, when they get into trouble, they resort to one thing: power. And all that does is magnify the problem. They'll overthrow. That off-speed pitch was what made Steve great, besides his killer instinct. But in order to be successful with a killer instinct, you've got to have the pitches. Well, he had three dandies. And he had them when he signed. I loved that. I didn't have to change anything. That's one of the things in coaching: if the pitcher has the pitches, you don't want to tinker with it just to put your stamp on it. The pitching takes care of any stamps you need.

The race went down to the final two games. We beat Houston 5-2 at Atlanta-Fulton County Stadium, and Smoltzie pitched a great game. So we're all sitting there knowing, okay, if L.A. wins its game, then we're going to L.A. for a one-game playoff; if they get beat, we're going to Pittsburgh for the championship series. There was no wild card then, and I wish there wasn't now. Most of the people stayed in the stadium after the game to watch the Dodgers play the Giants on the matrix board. We did, too. You don't know whether to jump up and down, or whether to sit there quietly. Because you're a little tight. We sat there on the edge of the infield and watched the game and hoped.

THE FIRST NLCS

The Giants beat the Dodgers 4-0, and we won the Western Division title in 1991. In one year, we went from worst to first. We played Pittsburgh in the playoffs, and the one thing I remember is our ability to handle Barry Bonds. We noticed that Barry had a tendency to swing for the fences once the playoffs rolled around. He was such a great hitter during the regular season, but we felt the bigger the game, the more he tried to pull the ball and jack it out of the park. We felt we could get him out down and away, that we could pitch him so that he could do everything *but* pull it. For some reason he never adjusted. He hit .148 in that series and didn't drive in a run. I don't know if it'd work today. But at that particular time in his career, we felt we could get him out down and away.

Bobby Cox kept us together all season by being the consistent manager that he is. By going about our business every day, by going out and getting organized and doing our work and going out and enjoying ourselves. If there was any pressure on him, you'd never know it. That's how he wanted his team to be. To be loose and enjoy what's going on. We went down 3-2 to Pittsburgh in the playoffs and had a team meeting. Bobby said, "We're going to win this thing. So let's just go out and play in a relaxed manner." It was a great thing to say. We were going to Pittsburgh and had a 21-year-old and a 22-year-old starting Games 6 and 7.

When he managed in a pennant race, Bobby managed the same way he did early in the season. His demeanor in the dugout didn't change between the first half and the second of the season. He does that. He's able to make you feel comfortable. He makes players feel comfortable in the dugout and in the clubhouse. He makes coaches feel comfortable. I've never been with a person who makes me feel good about myself the way that he does. And I think his players feel that way. Just by being himself. I don't think he has a set way; it's just what he is, what he's about.

Tommy lost Game 5 1-0. We sent Avery out to pitch Game 6. He pitched great. It was 0-0 at the end of the eighth inning, and Avery came in and said, "I'm done." I'm in panic city. It didn't even enter my mind that he might be done. I was thinking that he was going back out for the ninth. I went to Bobby and said, "Avery just said he's done."

Bobby goes, "What?"

I said, "Yeah, he says he's done."

He says, "Get Alejandro up real quick. What do you think?"

"Well, you have two choices," I said. "You can have a tired Avery in the ninth or a strong Alejandro Pena in the ninth. I think Av is just emotionally shot." He was just so gunned up, he hit a brick wall. And it didn't look like he'd hit a brick wall in the eighth; that's why it caught me by surprise.

So Alejandro comes in and he has Andy Van Slyke up with two outs. He just misses two home runs off the right field wall that are foul by a few inches. And Bobby is saying, "Where's that palm ball? Where's that palm ball?"

"He's gonna throw it here," I said. "He's gonna throw it here."

He kept pumping fastballs, and Van Slyke was hitting rockets foul. We had Stanton warming up and Bobby says, "I'm going to bring in Stanton to throw one pitch; I don't care. He's gotta mix in something."

Then, finally, the palm ball came in for called strike three. The off-speed pitch that Alejandro called the palm ball. He threw it like a palm ball, but it was like a change-up.

That took us to Game 7. Brian Hunter hit a three-run homer for us in the first. Smoltzie got out of trouble in the first. He had two runners on and two out, and somebody hit a drive to the base of the wall and it was caught.

Smoltzie came in and sat down. And he asked me, "Are you nervous?"

I said, "Well, are you?"

And he says, "No, I'm not nervous at all."

I said, "Well, then, I'm not either." I wanted to say, "Hell, yeah, I am."

Smoltzie pitched a complete-game 4-0 shutout. And we were going to the World Series.

THE FIRST WORLD SERIES

They say the 1991 World Series between us and the Minnesota Twins may be the greatest World Series ever played. All kinds of things went on: close games, controversial plays, great pitching. You'd be there thinking, "Oh, we've got them now." And then you don't. Then you had Jack Morris and 10 innings of shutout ball in Game 7, pitching out of numerous jams. And Smoltzie matching him pitch for pitch, when Morris was his idol growing up. You had two "worst to first" teams, so you had the enthusiasm in both cities. The pennant race and the NLCS were a lot more tense. I've always been able to enjoy the World Series games.

The Series was awesome. You felt so good about yourself, going through the pennant race and going through the NLCS. And then what happens? We have to get hooked up in all of these close games. These extra-inning games.

The Metrodome is as loud a joint as I've ever been in. I had to scream in the pitcher's ear when I went out on the mound. Being at home was real loud; the Chop Shop was one of the loudest places and one of the most intimidating places for a visiting team to come into. But the Metrodome was deafening. I wasn't particularly crazy about the field itself. It looks so odd with the garbage bags in center field. And then the roof—you couldn't find fly balls. I remember Bobby took the team out there and had the coaches just shoot rockets straight up, so that they could try to learn how to pick up the balls as they came out of the backdrop of the ceiling.

But the atmosphere was awesome. You sat in the dugout and it just shook. It actually shook from the noise. So if you think I was rocking just for the hell of it, I wasn't. I was getting pushed a little bit. In the end, I liked what John Schuerholz said: "They were the indoor champions and we were the outdoor champions." That's one way of looking at it. Even though we got beat, there wasn't a point in time where I ever thought we were losing that World Series. A lot of things cost us games. A particular pitch, not getting a runner in, something crazy like that.

Going into Game 6 we were up three games to two. It went into extra innings tied 3-3. In the 10th inning, we brought in Charlie Leibrandt to pitch in relief. Our feeling was that we had a 15-game winner sitting down there in the bullpen and that we might have to play awhile. So we brought him into the game. Our bullpen wasn't the strongest depth-wise, and we felt that Charlie's funky stuff, his off-speed stuff, would negate the power of the Twins' hitters, especially Kirby Puckett. If we had it to do over again today, we'd do it the same way. I thought it was a great idea. You're not bringing him in so he can hang a change-up; you're bringing him in so he can throw a change-up low and away and get the batter off balance. Of course, there's the human element in the game. Charlie didn't try to leave the change-up over the plate so Puckett could hit a home run to win the game. If he throws it down and gets a ground ball to retire the side, then it's "What a great move." I thought it was a great move regardless of the outcome. And we'd do it again.

After the game, Charlie was in the trainer's room. He was sitting on the floor by the table, pretty upset. So I went in. Charlie looked up and said, "How could I hang that pitch, Leo?"

"Charlie, we wouldn't be here without you," I said. "We wouldn't be here without your 15 wins. We wouldn't be here without your help with the young guys. There's a spread of food in there that's unbelievable. Get your ass up and let's go in there, have something to eat and a cold beer."

Charlie was such a stable guy, a real professional. You're gonna hurt when your emotions are riding high. But you get over it and move on. He just hung the change-up. I always tell pitchers this: it isn't the pitch that you throw; it's whatever you decided to throw, where did it end up? Believe me, make the selection and throw it with conviction. And if it ends up where you wanted it to end up, nobody's getting a hit.

That set up Game 7. It was tense. That's understating it. But we'd been in so many tense moments, you kind of get used to it. That was some game, Jack Morris against John Smoltz. Smoltzie was very relaxed in that game because it was the ultimate for him. He wasn't relaxed warming up, though. He started firing balls into the seats and everywhere else. After about six minutes, he looked at me and flipped me the ball and said, "I'm ready."

I said, "Are you sure?"

"Leo, I can't warm up any more," he said. "I gotta go out and pitch. This is wasted time."

We're enjoying that game on the bench. Oh, hell, yeah. Absolutely. You're just sitting there and you're going, "Wow!" Just to be a part of that, a part of that atmosphere. It's something you dreamed of when you were a little boy. And there you are. Right there. You know there are only two teams left playing. Nobody else in baseball is playing. You think about that. You try to win the game, but you enjoy it at the same time. The World Series is the ultimate as far as the players and the coaches and the front office enjoying the games. I feel that way. You enjoy being in the World Series. It's a son of a gun getting there. That's when you don't enjoy it near as much.

We had the chance to win it, but Lonnie Smith got fooled and hesitated at second on a hit that should have scored him. I still thought we were okay. I thought we'd get him in. One thing I try to do when I'm coaching is to focus completely on my area and leave the others alone. I concentrate on our pitchers. I can't remember who got the hit. I can't get upset about it or talk about it. I just know after that somebody popped out on a foul ball. Then they walked David Justice to load the bases with one out to pitch to Sid Bream. Sid hit a ground ball to first and they went first to home to first, double play.

Sure, it was disappointing. But it wasn't disheartening. You're proud of what you accomplished. I felt we were a better team than the Twins. But they were one run better in an extra-inning game. In a seven-game series. So that's cutting it pretty close.

Look at where Smoltz came from, from the first half of the season to Game 7. John started his reputation in the postseason right then and there. He pitched a great ballgame. It was nothing to nothing at the end of nine. Usually, as well as John pitched, that's good enough to win. Jack Morris kept gutting it up when we had the chance to score. And to do it for 10 innings?

Sometimes, you've just got to tip your hat.

A Trip to the Mound ...

All the Young Guns went through adversity in the 1991 season. Tommy had the trouble of giving up runs in the first inning. I remember one time he went something like seven or eight starts in a row where he gave up runs in the first inning. And after he got through the first, he would pitch extremely well. The sportswriters asked me if I was talking with Glavine about his first-inning problems. And I said no, he hears about it enough, he doesn't need to hear it from me. Besides, he was pitching well otherwise.

I thought it was circumstance: a bloop hit, a ground ball gets through, a broken bat hit. There was a game in San Diego where he went out and his mound presence was not the same. He was going out there not to win, but to not give up a run in the first inning. He'd already given up two and was in trouble. So I went out to the mound and I asked him if his arm hurt. He said no.

"Are you sure your arm isn't hurt?" I asked again.

"No," he said. "I'm telling you it doesn't hurt."

"Well," I said. "If your arm's not hurt and you can't throw the ball any better than that, we'll get somebody else in here who can." And then I turned and walked off the mound. As I got back to the dugout I thought, man, he is going to be pissed.

Tommy got the next out. He came in. He usually sits next to me, but in San Diego, he went clear down into the tunnel. Went on to pitch a great game and got the win. The next day in the outfield I went up to him and said, "Tommy, that was a great job last night."

He said, "Thanks, Leo."

"Let me ask you something," I said. "Did I piss you off?"

"Leo, out of the respect I have for our working relationship, I didn't tell you to go screw yourself right there on the mound," he said.

I smiled. "My goal was to make you mad."

"Well, it worked," he said. "Now that I've had time to think about it, I know where you were coming from."

"That was just coaching," I said. "Nothing personal."

You take many different avenues of approach. I could say that to Glavine, but I couldn't say that to Smoltz. With Smoltzie, at that particular time in his career, you had to take a lighter approach. Add a little humor into it. You need a lot of humor in this business, to be a pitching coach in the big leagues.

In Smoltzie's case, you would try to say the same thing, only have a lighter presentation. One time, I went out to the mound and I was gonna tell John to get his head out of his butt. I got out and he said, "Look, Leo, the catcher just came out and got on me. I don't need to be double-teamed."

I looked at him and said, "I'm sorry, John, I didn't know the catcher came out and got on your case. I agree you don't need to hear it from two people. I'm just gonna go on back to the dugout now."

SECOND INNING:

DÉJÀ VU ALL OVER AGAIN

oming into the 1992 season, we had our heads held up higher. I'll never forget: we're in West Palm Beach, playing the Dodgers in a spring training game, and Avery's starting. The place is sold out, and here we go again. He strikes out the first guy he faces. You can feel the intensity level … in a spring training game. That's the first time I'd ever experienced that. And here the thing starts all over again. You get the feeling back. You feel like you're playing a regular-season game in a pennant race, and all you're doing is playing a spring training game.

We got off to a slow start in 1992. We were 20-27 in late May, and you start thinking, what's going on here? Let's go! And all of a sudden, we started firing shutouts. We had 24 shutouts that season, set a Braves record for consecutive scoreless innings.

During one stretch in July, we were on fire and won 21 out of 24. Smoltz went 4-1 during that streak. The loss? To the Cubs, against some pitcher named Greg Maddux. During that same time, Glavine went 5-0. You know what that's called in baseball? That's called *dealing*. They were both *dealing*. In the first year, 1991, you talked in terms of being a "good rotation" and "everything coming together." Now, you started thinking in terms of "great rotation." Those guys were *dealing*, man. You're looking at all the shutouts and the way they're pitching, and you're thinking to yourself: This is a great rotation. And other people started talking about it using those terms.

In '92, I was walking tall. Every day I stepped out of that bullpen with a starting pitcher who had pitched great in a playoff and in the World Series. That makes you feel real good. And the pitcher feels good about himself. The things is, to be great you have to do it over a period of time; you can't just be a one-year shot. It means more when you sustain it. And the way they pitched in '92 was unbelievable in terms of just completely shutting people down. We led the league in ERA that season with 3.14, the first time the Braves had done that since 1958. We led the league in shutouts. The thing I was most proud of was the innings pitched by our starting rotation. You can't accomplish any of those other things if you're not going to the post.

Tommy went out and pitched when he didn't feel good. His arm was bothering him some, but he still went to the post and that's what separates great pitchers from mediocrity. He finished 20-8 with a 2.76 ERA. Avery wasn't quite as good as he was the year before, but he was better than his 11-11 record. Smoltzie had a great ERA, 2.85, and was 15-12. And Charlie had another one of his 15-win years.

All we were doing that season was focusing on repeating, doing it all over again. The excitement and the enthusiasm were still there, the newness of it. That didn't change in '92. We had a powerhouse club in '92. That season was a steady-as-she-goes season, take the lead and then shut down the opposition. You start to become a machine, a juggernaut going through the National League. We started getting into people's heads. You'd look at the opposition when we were trotting out there to start a game, and you could see them going, "Oh, no."

BACK TO PITTSBURGH

In the NLCS, here we go again, it's Pittsburgh. And it's another battle. We played a couple during the playoffs against Pittsburgh, we played a day game in Atlanta, and I called down to the bullpen. I didn't recognize the voice of the person who picked up. "Who is this?" I said.

"This is Bob Walk."

I'd reached the Pirates' dugout; somehow, the wires were crossed. I said, "What the hell am I doing talking to you?"

He goes, "Well, who is this?"

"This is Leo."

"Well, what the hell are you doing calling over here?"

We went up three games to one; then Pittsburgh came back and tied the series. Now we're down and here we are: Game 7. I ran into Jim Leyland, the Pirates manager, in the tunnel prior to that game. "Oh, my God, Leo, I can't take this," he said. "I can't take it."

SMOLTZ WAS NAMED THE MOST VALUABLE PLAYER OF THE 1992 NLCS.

"Me neither," I said. Because all the games were close. Pittsburgh and Atlanta were very evenly matched. Our pitchers held them in check again. Bonds batted .261 for the series, and the team batting average was .255.

I don't think there's ever been a better moment than Game 7s. Doug Drabek had a 2-0 shutout going into the ninth when Terry Pendleton leads off with a double to right. That brings up David Justice, who hits a grounder to second. And their second baseman, Jose Lind, makes an error. He was automatic, only six errors in the regular season, a Gold Glover. And he boots the ground ball. I'm thinking, this is unbelievable. And it just kept going. Drabek walks Sid Bream to load the bases. We hit a sacrifice fly to cut the lead to 2-1. They bring in Stan Belinda to pitch. The bases are loaded when Francisco Cabrera comes up to pinch hit.

That's just a moment in time. You think about it now and everything stops. You see Sid Bream off second base. Hoping Belinda would get behind in the count and have to throw Frankie a fastball. He'd already hit a bullet off Belinda that went foul. And then he got it through that hole. And you're thinking, "Oh, my God! Oh, my God!" You're sitting there and you're tongue-tied in the dugout. You're watching the play, but you can't say anything. You can't scream, you can't say "Oh, my God." You just have to watch it develop. And then once Bream crosses the plate, once the call is made, then all the emotions spill forth.

We still had the newness, still had the taste, in '92. And then when you have Sid Bream scoring, what we did was absolutely magical. Believe me, the Chop Shop was shaking that night. I could feel our dugout shaking from the noise and the excitement. I remember Andy Van Slyke and Barry Bonds sitting in the outfield on their butts going, "Oh, no." I just kind of stood there and stared. If you'll notice, I'm not in that picture where they're running out on the field. I sat there in the dugout stunned. So I could imagine how they felt in that other dugout.

THE SECOND WORLD SERIES

Tommy Glavine pitched a great game in the first game of the Series, beating Jack Morris. In the second game, we had a one-run lead in the ninth, and Ed Sprague hit a two-run homer off our closer, Jeff Reardon. Unfortunately, it happened to Reardon again in Game 3. He came in with the bases loaded and the score tied in the ninth and gave up a game-winning hit. We'd picked up Reardon late in the season after Alejandro Pena got hurt. He was one of the premier closers in history. We felt that even if he'd lost a little off his stuff, he could still get by on know-how and guts. And he did some great things for us in a short period of time.

Reardon was a good matchup for Sprague. The Sprague home run was just a pitch that Reardon threw up and out over the plate. I'm sure it bothered him a lot. But he was very professional and very businesslike, a great guy. He just made a mistake up in the zone. That turned that series around. We would have been up two games to none. Going to Toronto.

That's when people started complaining about our bullpen. And one reason was because the starting pitching was so good. I never thought we had a bad bullpen in the 12 years we've been here. Any little screw-up at all, it was magnified because of our starting rotation.

In the final game, it was tied at 2-2 in the 11th inning. Just like in the '91 Series, we brought in Charlie Leibrandt to pitch. We had Reardon warming up. But we couldn't bring Reardon in after what had already happened in the Series. Dave Winfield hit that double to win the Series. I can barely remember that. That's one of the years I can't really remember.

The things I remember the most about '92 are all the shutouts and the juggernaut of the Atlanta Braves going through the National League. And then the Pirates and Sid Bream.

Tommy was 20-8 that year. But he lost the Cy Young Award to a guy named Greg Maddux, who happened to be a free agent. And I'd make the case that Maddux was about to become the greatest free agent signing in the history of the game.

THIRD INNING:
MAD DOG'S ARRIVAL

In the off season after 1992, the Braves were looking to land an impact free agent, and there were only two names we considered: Barry Bonds and Greg Maddux. I had my fingers crossed. I knew that Bobby wanted Maddux real bad. We took a vote and Maddux came out as the one we should go after. My thought was that you can never have enough great pitching. If you have great starting pitching, you can always figure out something toward the end of the game. If you don't have it, I don't care how smart you are, you're not going to figure anything out just trying to catch up.

And to add a great pitcher to an already great pitching rotation? Can you imagine adding Greg Maddux to a starting rotation that had already thrown 24 shutouts the previous year? Now *that's* when you're never going to get into a losing streak. Very seldom will those four starters run out there and every one of them lose.

MADDUX'S CAREER NUMBERS PUT HIM IN THE SAME SENTENCE AS LEGENDS SUCH AS WALTER JOHNSON AND CY YOUNG.

When you looked at Maddux across the way when he was with the Cubs, you really wanted to kick his butt. Because he's cocky, he's sneaky and you knew by looking at his face that he was outsmarting you. He was another killer. Tremendous competitor. Nobody liked him. Everybody said, let's get this SOB. He was one of the greatest pitchers I'd ever seen. Got to coach him in the All-Star Game in '92. I remember getting into the elevator with him and saying, "Hey, man, you're a great pitcher."

And he said, "Thanks." That's all I said; that's all he said. He probably thought, "A coach blowing smoke up my butt." When I heard the organization talking about the possibility of getting Greg Maddux, I thought, oh, my golly; you add that to the pitching staff that's already in place, we're really gonna be *dealing*."

He signed with the Braves and took less money than the Yankees offered him. For one thing, he wanted to stay in the National League. I think the city, the environment, had a whole lot to do with his decision. Mad Dog doesn't like all the hubbub of New York. He's going into the Hall of Fame, but he doesn't like the accolades and all that stuff, and he never talks about himself. He's quiet, but don't let that fool you. He'll cut your heart out in a minute.

When he first got to Atlanta, Mad Dog came up to me and said, "I just want you to know that I give up a lot of 0-2 hits."

"What are you talking about?" I asked

"Well, 0-2 is the most vulnerable count a hitter can have, no balls and two strikes," he said. "And I'm going to try to take him out immediately."

**WALKING IN FROM THE BULLPEN AT TURNER FIELD:
EDDIE PEREZ, MAZZONE AND MADDUX.**

"That sounds good to me," I said.

"Be sure you tell Bobby that," he said. "I don't want him getting upset."

I went to Bobby and said, "Maddux wanted me to tell you something. He's going to give up a lot of 0-2 hits."

"What?" Bobby said. "What the hell are you talking about?"

"Well, he told me no balls and two strikes is the most vulnerable count a hitter can have," I said. "And he's going to take him out immediately."

Bobby looks at me and goes, "Well, Leo, that's what separates mediocrity from greatness."

To my thinking, 1993 was the greatest starting four: Maddux, Glavine, Smoltz and Avery. All four won at least 15 games, the first time a Braves team had ever done that.

When you looking at those starters, you're going to see a common denominator. Maddux finished 20-10 with a 2.36 ERA. He won the Cy Young Award for the second year in a row. Maddux has a sinker, change-up, a cut fastball and an occasional curve. His best pitches are his sinker and change-up. He can work both sides of the plate with all his pitches. He's basically down and away with right-handed hitters, and he works both sides with left-handed hitters. He has great movement on the ball, on both sides of the plate.

Those are his pitches and he throws them with great control. I mean *pinpoint* control. He says if he's got his fastball going and changing speeds, that's all he needs. He has a very simple plan: he wants them to hit it on the handle or the end of the bat. That's very important; he *wants* them to hit it. There are a lot of pitchers who pitch away from contact, and they don't have much success.

Glavine was 22-6 with a 3.20 ERA. When you talk about him, you're talking fastball, change-up, slider, occasional curve and living on the down and away strike—and never giving in. A lot of opposing managers have told me that they know where he's going to be and they still can't do anything about it. He's stubborn, and he stays stubborn on the edge of the plate.

He has beautiful mechanics that he can repeat. And repeat, and repeat, and repeat. Tommy has a tremendous motion in terms of not being able to pick up a change of speeds. Even when you know it's coming, you can't pick it up. He's just your classic left-hander. I've seen Tommy pitch great games, like a 1-0 shutout at Enron Field, which is just a brutal park for pitchers. Never threw one breaking ball. All fastballs and change-ups. I think the only time Tommy gets in trouble is when he's trying to decide how much effort to put into the pitch.

Then you have Smoltzie, who was 15-11 that year, 3.62 ERA. He has the best stuff of all of them. Greatest slider I've ever seen from a right-handed pitcher. Powerful fastball. A nasty split-finger. A change-up. And a curveball. And later on in his career, he even threw a knuckleball. There's not a pitch invented that he can't throw. Or an arm angle invented that he can't execute. He's done all those things. But it takes one thing a lot of pitchers can't do: they can't trust it. It takes the courage to trust it, that it's going to work.

John's always had good control. I remember in the early part of the '90s, the only time he ever got hurt was on a two-strike breaking ball. He'd try to bounce it in the dirt, and that's when he'd leave it up in the zone. That's the only thing I can ever remember him getting hurt on. Great stuff. Classic delivery. Great athlete.

And then Steve Avery. 18-6, 2.94 ERA. Fastball. Change-up. Curveball. Killer. Pull the hat down and let's go. An attacker. Now all four pitchers we're talking about are attackers in different ways. Avery shows it a little more. Steve had a four-seam fastball. His change-up, he threw it hard. A lot of teams thought he was sinking the ball; it was actually his change-up. He also had a good breaking ball. Steve was able to have success because he trusted a change of speeds at an age most pitchers wouldn't. Especially if, like him, you're signed out of high school as a power pitcher.

And what's the common denominator? The down and away strike. And innings pitched. Three out of the top four pitchers with the most innings pitched in the National League that year were from Atlanta: Maddux, Smoltz and Glavine.

Glav and Maddux were both 27 years old in '93. Avery was 23. Smoltz was 26. I'll tell you what, you felt pretty good coming in from that bullpen with those guys. It made you feel proud and you walked with your head high. You know what? The opposition knew it too. I remember going into Chicago after Maddux signed with us. Mark Grace and Shawon Dunston were stretching behind the batting cage, and I'm always out in the park early watching the other team hit.

And they go, "There's Leo with a big grin on his face. Who you got pitching today, Leo?"

"Well, Glavine's pitching today," I said.

"What about tomorrow?"

"Maddux."

"Well, how about the next day?"

"Smoltz."

"Well, who you got left for the fourth game of the series?"

"Avery."

And they just shook their heads. And walked away.

INTO THE FIRE

That was the year we had the incredible pennant race with San Francisco. We were something like 10 games back at the break, and at the All-Star Game Barry Bonds was telling our pitchers that it was over. He told Smoltzie and all of them, "Man, the race is over; you can't catch us."

That was the last great pennant race in baseball, because that was the last year before the introduction of the wild card team. It really started when we picked up Fred McGriff on July 20. There were a lot of people in baseball who said we got McGriff too late, that we couldn't catch the Giants. But I think what people might not have understood is that our starting pitching was that good. And having that one extra bat was going to make all the difference in the world. Before McGriff's first game, a luxury box next to the press box blew up. I have that picture. Jeff Blauser and Lemke are standing there and it's blazing behind them. It sounded like a bomb went off, and we all took off for the right field wall. We were down 5-0 that night. Blauser hit a three-run homer; then McGriff hit a two-run homer. And we were off and running.

We had a big series in San Francisco in August and were still seven and a half games back. We got out there for that series and Avery said, "Aw, Leo, we're in great shape."

"Good," I said. "I'm glad you think so. What makes you say that?"

He said, "Well, if you read the papers, Burkett and Swift are the two big starters. They're past the 150-inning mark and they're talking about getting tired. We get past the 150-inning mark and we're just kicking in. Don't worry, we'll catch them."

I said, "Well, I feel a helluva lot better, Av, since you've told me that."

I remember that Robbie Thompson, the second baseman for the Giants, used to always sit over there in the dugout at Candlestick and mock me rocking in the dugout. He even did it in the on-deck circle one time. That was a very good Giant team. They were still in Candlestick Park, and it was a miserable place. But it's a lot better than Toledo or Pawtucket. Somebody said once they didn't like the warmup mound. And I said, "Well, we can always go down to one of these farm clubs and warm up on that mound and see if you like it there."

We swept them. Avery won 5-3 in the first game. He was throwing 88-89 mph. We got the lead and in the eighth and ninth innings, he was throwing 92-93 mph. The last two innings of that game, he threw all fastballs. Then Glavine won 6-4. I'll never forget; the game was tied 2-2 in the fifth inning. Will Clark was up to bat with the bases loaded, and he is in my Top 10 of toughest clutch hitters we've ever faced. And Tommy got Will Clark to roll over on a change-up for a ground-ball double play. Lefty to lefty, down and away. That got us out of deep trouble, and then we went on to win the game. Then Maddux won 9-1. We scored a ton of runs early and then he just shut them down.

One of the best things that happened for us that year was Greg McMichael. Mac was great, a 2.06 ERA and 19 saves. I didn't know anything about him before spring training. Mac was one of the invitees on Field Two. As is the Braves way, every pitcher that comes to spring training gets to pitch. So McMichael comes in and has a one-two-three inning. We play another game, he comes in and has another one-two-three inning with a pretty good change-up.

He graduated from Field Two to Field One and started pitching against the better hitters. We had it set up so that he would pitch before the other team made substitutions and brought in their Double-A and Triple-A guys at the end of the game. He did great. So we decided to put him in against the Mets to face their top left-handers. We had him go up against Darryl Strawberry and Keith Hernandez. He not only retired the side, he made them look sick. Mac's walking off the field and Terry Pendleton, our third baseman, comes over and he looks at me and says, "If you guys don't pick him on this pitching staff, you ought to be shot."

And so now we're going to play the Yankees. We had him pitch against Wade Boggs and Mattingly, and he made them look sick with his change-up. Nobody could hit him. Mac made the club, and for the next four years he was a huge part of our success as a setup guy and a closer. McMichael's pitch was the change-up. And he could make it break a couple of ways. He was the guy we brought in to face left-handed hitters, and he was right-handed. He was tremendous. And Terry Pendleton aided us in our decision-making.

We had to win 104 games that year. And that's just to get into the playoffs. The last day was just like 1991. We beat Colorado. San Francisco, ironically enough, lost to the Dodgers. The Giants won 103 games and didn't get in.

That was a great pennant race. That was the year they got Bonds and we got Maddux. I think it worked out pretty good. For both sides.

AN OLD-SCHOOL SERIES

We played Philadelphia in the NLCS, and, you know, here we go again: all one-run games. The thing I remember about that '93 Phillies team is that their hitters had a way of fighting off our best pitches. If we made the out pitch we wanted, they would either tip it or nick it or fight it off or push it away or foul it off. I talked to Lenny Dykstra about that once. I asked him, "Lenny, how were you guys able to do that?"

"We had a saying in the clubhouse," he said. "Keep your nose on the ball. We hated the Braves so much. We were sick and tired of hearing about the Braves, and how good they are." And they had a group of guys who were nasty: John Kruk, Dykstra, Darren Dalton, Wally Backman and Dave Hollins. When I say "nasty bunch" I'm giving them a great compliment. They were from the old school, they were like the Gashouse Gang. And they played us tough.

One reason we got beat was Maddux got hit with a line drive in the sixth game. He got hit on the leg in the first inning or two. Bobby looked at me and asked what I thought.

"Well, he's better on one leg than most pitchers are on two," I said. "I don't think we have any choice but to keep him in."

We had great starting pitching in that series. We allowed 19 runs, and the Phillies allowed 29. But we lost in six. Were we were out of gas from the pennant race? I don't know. I didn't sense that when I was in the dugout. Not at all. The pitchers didn't run out of gas. It's hard to say if that was a factor. I really think you have to play games, and you have to execute and get people out.

Two good teams played a best-of-seven league championship series and both of them played well. I think their hitters were able to fight off more of our pitchers. It was a gritty club we played, a tough club. And we were the same way. We lost Game 5 by a few inches in the ninth inning when Lemke hit a line shot down the left field line and it went foul. In the top of the next inning, the 10th, we thought we had Dykstra struck out and he hit a home run into center field against Wohlers. So factors like that lead to winning and losing. I think it was just a matter of two good teams playing, and one of them had to win and one of them had to lose.

I remember sitting in the dugout and we were one out away from getting eliminated. I looked at one of the pitchers and said, "We're cutting this kind of close, aren't we?" You've got to throw a sense of humor in there because if you don't, it'll drive you crazy. It was very disappointing. You can take losing a World Series. It's very difficult to handle not getting *into* the World Series when you have the opportunity. As far as I'm concerned, that was two great teams playing one another and nobody gave away anything.

The final game was in Philly, and after we got beat, we were trying to get back to the hotel on the bus. And that bus was rocking. Fans were banging on it and rocking it, actually rocking it. I like to rock, but this was ridiculous. And pelting us with rocks and stuff. They were happy campers.

That Philly team might have been the best lineup we've faced all these years, as far as fighting our pitches off and making us work harder for the end result. You look at the stats and none of our starters threw eight or nine innings. That particular lineup was able to get our pitch counts up from what they normally were, so fatigue became a factor for our pitching staff, which made the pitchers you would not normally use come into play. You had to cover that extra inning or two. And that's probably the reason why we lost to the Phillies.

THE UNWELCOME SEASON

After the 1993 season, I felt like 1994 was going to be our season. But I've felt it was going to be the year every year since 1991. I've felt we've had the greatest starting rotation of anybody in the game every year. That's never changed. I think the hunger stays the same all the time.

We got off to a 13-1 start, highlighted by Kent Mercker's 6-0 no-hitter against the Dodgers on April 8. After the seventh inning of that game, he came into the dugout and said, "I'm tired."

"Are you nuts?" I said.

He goes, "What do you mean?"

"Look up at the scoreboard," I said.

And he looked up and it wasn't that he didn't know he had a no-hitter going; he'd lost track of the innings. It was the end of the seventh and he thought it was only the end of the sixth.

And I said, "Are you out of your mind? You've got a chance to throw a no-hitter, what's wrong with you?"

Once he found out he only had two innings to go rather than three, he said, "Oh, I feel pretty good now." And he got it. I think he got it with 131 pitches. That was Mercker's best year with us.

We started off hot, but we kind of leveled off. Montreal had a good club that year, and our bullpen was shaky. The bottom line is we didn't get to finish the season anyway. We were six games behind Montreal when the strike happened. I think we would have caught them. When it stops like that, it just makes you sick. And then they cancelled the World Series.

It makes you sick to your stomach. I was angry. I always thought, "They'll get it done. We might miss a game or two, but they'll get something done." And you just sat there and it just made you sick.

In the final weeks of the season, you just tried to be locked in on the game once it started. But once the game was over, that's all anybody talked about in the clubhouse. It wasn't how we were going to pitch this guy or that guy; it was about, "Well, are we through now? Is the season over?" It was tough. It was miserable when it happened. It's unbelievable. You go to the ballpark and there's no game.

Of course, Tommy was a leader in the union. All he was doing was his job. When you give Tommy Glavine a job to do, he's going to do it and get it done right. I didn't realize they were going to strike until the last game in Colorado. I thought they would get it figured out and continue. Or they'd get it settled and we'd go right into the postseason; they'd set up a playoff series to see who went to the World Series and I knew we'd be in it. I thought they'd pick it up in late September or October. I figured they might cancel the rest of the games; no way in hell did I think they'd cancel the season.

The last game in Colorado, I remember asking Mad Dog, "Are you tired?" Because you really have to exert yourself in Colorado to make the ball do something.

And he said, "It don't really matter, I'll be on a plane in the morning. I won't be pitching for a while. So I'll go ahead and pitch while I'm tired." And he was just being honest. Maddux threw a shutout, and the next day, there was no game. As a matter of fact, I think Mad Dog left for his home in Vegas right after that game. Then we came back to Atlanta, and I'd still go to the park at two or three o'clock in the afternoon. And there'd be no game. And you'd go and get on the treadmill or something. It was ridiculous.

You go eight or nine months, seven days a week. Be at the ballpark at one o'clock until after midnight. On the road. As soon as your season is over, there's such a finality. The year of the strike, it was over and you weren't anywhere. You're sitting there in your home at three o'clock in the afternoon and you get depressed. On top of everything else, it's such an abrupt change in your lifestyle.

No matter what happens in a season, at least you know if you've won or you've lost. With the strike, nobody wins. Everybody loses. Especially the good people who are in the seats. And then to have to listen to all the BS just drives you crazy.

When the players went out on strike on August 12, we were six games behind Montreal. I'll never forget, Kevin Malone was the general manager of Montreal and he popped his gums saying that they were the division champs. And I remember the next year when we resumed play and went to Montreal, Bobby Cox made it a point to find Kevin Malone and tell him that we were only six games out when the season shut down and had every intention of winning the division. That nobody could declare anyone division champs because the season wasn't completed. Bobby found him and let him know it. We'd been in that position before where we had to catch somebody. To us, our attitude was that we were not in that difficult of a situation.

That whole thing was sad. What was even sadder was having to go through with all the replacement players the next spring. That was dark. From the strike date of '94 to the first spring training of 1995, it was awfully hard. Brutal. You didn't feel good about anything. About yourself, about baseball, nothing. And then to have to listen to all the BS just drove you crazy. When they settled, everybody thought thank God, we've got our players back. We couldn't wait. There was no champion in '94. There was no World Series, which broke everybody's heart. Then in '95, you go in and there's no spring training. You're beginning to wonder what in the world is going on.

When we started that season up in '95, that might have been one of the happiest moments in everybody's careers.

A Trip to the Mound ...

I'll never forget the first practice session I had with Greg Maddux. He was throwing balls in the dirt. He was high, up and in, up and away, off target. As a coach, you're just observing. It's your first session. You're checking him out. And he turned around and looked at me and said, "What'd you think of that session?"

And I said, "To be perfectly honest with you, I didn't think it was that good."

He goes, "I didn't either."

He was testing me, trying to find out if I'd be a coach that said, "Oh, everything's fine" and all the clichés. But my basic approach was just to be honest with him. The next day, there was a tremendous amount of improvement in his control. So I was already making him better! I've always said, he won a Cy Young before he came to the Braves and then he won three in a row after he got here. So I know one thing: as his pitching coach, I sure didn't mess him up.

Once I got to watch him every day, he was greater than I ever expected. You don't realize how good his control is until you sit behind him, watch him practice and then watch him pitch. When he was with the Cubs, you'd look over and think, *man*, that guy's got good control. But when you stand behind him and watch him on a daily basis, it boggles your mind. It really does. He gets upset if he's off an inch, whereas most pitchers are completely happy if they're that close.

He'd always turn around with every pitch and say, "That's a strike, that's a ball." Now, with the fluctuation of the strike zone as it's evolved in recent years, he'll say, "That *used* to be a strike."

Most of our starters were home-grown. They came up through the system we'd put in place. We didn't have to sell our philosophy to Mad Dog because his philosophy was the same. There was a misconception that he pitched inside a lot. What he really wanted to do was to come in down and away so that he could then go inside whenever he wanted. And he very rarely pitched right-handed batters in. It was left-handed hitters he'd pitch in with his cutter and then come back with his two-seam comeback fastball to freeze them. If you'll notice, he very rarely starts a hitter off with a pitch inside. It's always down and away. So there wasn't any selling at all.

And he had no problem with the throwing program. He didn't throw as much as Smoltz, Glav or Avery. If he felt real good with his pitches, he didn't throw as much. If he didn't feel real good about his pitches, then he threw more. Whereas the other guys did it on a very consistent basis and never changed, regardless of how they felt.

I'd be a fool to make him change or do something he wasn't comfortable doing. I think he liked what we offered in terms of pitching philosophy, the manager, the organization. And we *loved* what he offered because he taught us a great deal, too. I've used a tremendous number of his ideas over the years, such as getting your alignment on the pitching rubber, getting the right direction to the strike zone. There's so much more: recognizing what hitters are trying to do, pitching mechanics, the whole ball of wax. Especially the preparation.

Just to give an example, we were having our meeting going over the Yankees before the '96 World Series. We were going over their offense and I was reading our advance scouting report and got to Bernie Williams. And he interrupted me and said, "That report's not right. I've been watching film on him for a week. And that report's not right."

So I looked at the team and said, "Did everybody hear what Mad Dog said? Okay, screw this report. We all go with what Maddux says."

Greg Maddux is the first pitcher I ever coached that told me a hitter was in trouble after he'd faced him one time in a game. He said, "That guy's in deep trouble if he comes up in the seventh or eighth inning with the tying run at second base." He sets them up. He pitches them one way in order to set them up for later. He's like a poker player. He doesn't play his hand all the time.

When he came to spring training with us for the first time, he said, "Don't get all messed up over my pitch selection. I'm going to pitch everybody backwards in spring training. Because there are scouts up in the stands charting what I do."

He remembers hitters and what they did. I remember he threw a shutout in Montreal. His start before that, he had a 3-2 lead against the Cardinals in the ninth inning and Todd Zeile got a hit to tie it with two out and a man on second. In the game in Montreal, he had a one-run lead and he was in the same situation—man on second in the ninth inning. The guy hit a ground ball to short, we threw him out and we had a shutout. We're shaking hands as he's coming off the mound and he says, "Now if I'd located like that against Zeile in my last start, I would have won that game, too."

Mad Dog never forgets what hitters have done against him in the past. They talk about Bonds hitting home runs off him and the first thing he'll say is, "Well, check how many men were on base when he hit them. And find out how many home runs he's hit off me after the fifth inning."

I could go on and on about Greg Maddux. But the best way to put it is that he's the greatest pitcher I've ever seen. More pitchers would have greater success if they studied Mad Dog's thought processes, his preparation and this competitiveness and how he takes care of all the intangibles. Greg Maddux is a great example of a Johnny Sain-ism: you gotta work hard, but you've gotta work smart. That's the Sain-ism you think of with Greg Maddux. He's just the greatest pitcher I've ever seen. I'm still in awe when he practices and I watch his control. After 10 years.

One time we were playing the Yankees in interleague play and Bobby went to the mound. He wanted to know if Maddux wanted to walk Jorge Posada and pitch to Scott Brosius. Mad Dog says, "Give me two pitches to Posada. If I get behind 2-0, I'll walk him. But I think I'll get him to pop up to third."

So Bobby came in from the mound and I said, "What happened?"

"Well, he thinks he can get him to pop up to third."

"What?"

"Yeah, but if he gets behind in the count 2-0, he's gonna walk him." Bobby kind of shrugged. "Hell, Leo, I went out there to tell him to walk Posada and pitch to Brosius. But he says he can do this, so let's see."

I said, "Well, I know what he's going to throw. He's going to throw a cutter up and in off the plate." And he did. Second pitch. Posasda popped up to third base.

There was the time we'd gone three months into the season and I hadn't been to the mound to talk to him all year. So before the game, he asked me about that. Had I been out to the mound? I said no. He said, "Well, it gets kind of lonely out there. I'll look in during the sixth inning, so come on out and pay me a visit."

Sure as hell, in the sixth inning he looks into the dugout and Bobby says, "Hey, Mad Dog's looking in. Something must be wrong. Go check it out."

I run out to the mound and say, "Mad Dog, you're pitching a great game."

"Yeah, I feel good," he says. "Everything's going fine." We shoot the bull for a minute, and he says, "Okay, we've got your TV time now. Thanks for coming out. You know, sometimes it helps just to talk to somebody."

I went back in and Bobby asked what was the matter. And I said, "Oh, nothing. His heart was racing a little bit. He just needed to calm down."

FOURTH INNING:

THE CHAMPIONSHIP SEASON

Like I said, our expectation every year since 1991 has been to win the World Series.

And if we don't get to the World Series and win it, then we've fallen short of our goal. I'd much rather have that standard to live up to and try to accomplish than to have to say every year that we're rebuilding or we hope to get to .500 this season.

Bobby Cox never gets enough credit for how we have sustained this 12-year run. In the baseball world, there's not a soul that wouldn't come around and tell you that he is a first-class manager. There's a tremendous number of accolades given to him within the baseball world. But you have your second-guessers, and I guess they're going to second-guess him all the way to the Hall of Fame. I don't think he loses any sleep over it.

On the outside, people perceive things the way they want. Johnny Sain told me something: there's a tremendous number of people who have the answer *after the fact*; there are very few who have it *before*.

What's remarkable about Bobby is his professionalism and how he treats people. There's no phony act to him. If he's going to talk to a player, he doesn't do anything in the press. He's always said it's about the players, not about anything else. The players know that he's for them. The players also know that if the rules aren't kept, the certain rules he has, then they're going to hear about it. A lot of times when they hear about it, nobody else knew about it. He's just a class act.

Bobby is the one who gave me my opportunity. He gave me a lot of responsibility over the pitching when he became the general manager. I'd been in the minor leagues a long time, and that's when I first felt that at some point in time I was going to be a major-league pitching coach. He gave me a lot of leeway and allowed me to use the programs I wanted to use. He and the scouting department signed all these pitchers.

When John Smoltz was sent to the big leagues in 1988, we were all in the clubhouse in Richmond after the game. Bobby said he needed three tickets to Shea Stadium for John's major-league debut. The general manager of Richmond said, "I know you're going and I know Smoltz is going. What do we need a third ticket for?"

Bobby said, "I want Leo there for John's major-league debut."

That's the best thing anybody has ever done for me to show me their appreciation. The second best thing was when he named me pitching coach. Sending me to New York showed

SMOLTZ HAS ONE OF THE MOST BEAUTIFUL DELIVERIES IN THE
GAME.

so much class. And from that day forward, I was going to do anything I could to help him get the job done. I haven't heard of very many people who have done something like that, especially in this business.

For him to become the manager down on the field and for me to be the pitching coach, that's just my perfect scenario, because we'd worked so closely since 1986 to get all this pitching ready. We've had very few and miniscule disagreements. Every once in a while, I'll get a little message to not do this, or to do that a little different way. But it's very subtle and nobody else knows about it. There are a lot of times when we have a lot of fun on the bench. And you've got to have somebody to talk to. So Bobby will look over and say, "Well, Leo, you got any chest pains yet?"

"Well, yeah. How 'bout you?"

"Well, the top of my head feels like it's going to blow off."

"I just hope we can make it through nine."

We want to win so bad. And we pull for the players, we pull for the team and the organization. It's not a phony act; it's real. It's a lot of fun. I always call it good stress because it gets your juices going. I want to tell you: the bigger the crowd and the louder the crowd, the more excitement.

Our pitching staff led the league in ERA in 1995 for the third straight year, the first time that's happened since the Baltimore Orioles did it from 1969 to 1972. And Mad Dog won his fourth straight Cy Young Award. He won 19 games and walked just 23 guys. He nearly walked fewer batters than his number of wins; I mean, that's just unheard of. I remember him pitching a game that year, and he never missed his target one time. Guys are going to be off target periodically. But I've never seen a guy go through a full season and hit a target like that on such a consistent basis. What's incredible is that Mad Dog didn't sacrifice control. He still worked the edges of the plate, not giving into the middle just because he didn't want to walk anybody. He had streaks of 60 or 80 batters without a walk. One ended against the opposing pitcher. You know what the sad part is? It was a borderline pitch.

I've never seen a better two-season run than Maddux had in 1995 and 1996. John Smoltz in '96 was as dominant and as awesome a pitcher as I've ever seen. Tom Glavine in '91 was the same way. But there were some ups and downs. Small ones, but some. But in Maddux's run over those two years, there weren't any. I remember seeing a poster at Atlanta-Fulton County Stadium that said: Auto-Maddux. And he was. His ERAs for those two years were 1.56 and 1.63. Unbelievable.

Avery hurt his side that year; his record was 7-13. It was a little bit mysterious because Steve would never complain about injuries. He didn't go into the trainer's room much. It was that type of mentality that allowed him to be very good. I'm sure he was in a lot more pain than he was letting on. Steve's a great competitor, and he continued to perform. I think he pitched better than his win-loss record indicated, so we stuck with him because of that and because he'd been too good to us in the past.

That was the year that Mark Wohlers emerged as our closer. He had blossomed into the role, and he had great stuff: 100-mph fastballs, 89-mph splits and nasty sliders. His control was good. You pretty much knew when he came in that it was lights out. He was really a dominant closer there for a few years. My approach with him wasn't really any different than it was with anybody else, except my presentations to Mark would be a little bit more on the lighter side. He's an emotional guy. The reason they made him a reliever in the minor leagues was because he worried himself to death too much in between starts. But when he came to the ballpark not knowing when he was going to pitch, he picked up speed on his fastball because he was able to not think about things so much. He could let his natural abilities take over.

That was the first year of the three-division system and the wild card. We finished 21 games in front and had the most wins in the National League. And then we had to go to Colorado for the best-of-five division series. That's the year that stress levels became higher, headaches became more prevalent, your belly started to hurt more, blood pressure went high. And it was for one simple reason: the extra playoff series and because it's only a best-of-five. I think that detracts and takes away from everything you've accomplished over a full season.

There's so much I dislike about the best-of-five format. Baseball is a sport where you win over the long haul. You win 90 games, you win 100 games. Then by some flukish thing, you can end up getting knocked off in a best-of-five. It negates the depth of your ball club, which is the reason why you won in the first place. One little freaky thing can happen and you're knocked out, and all of a sudden everything you've done over the season doesn't matter. We've won most of our best-of-fives; we got knocked out twice. But it's a joke. There's never been a baseball champion determined in the history of the game except in a best-of-seven series. Then all of a sudden you throw a best-of-five in there.

Colorado had home-field advantage. That doesn't make any sense at all. They were the wild card, won 77 games. Where's your reward for winning your division? We have to go to Coors

Field and I'm sitting there thinking, please, let's hold them to five runs or less. You know, that's a lousy way to have to coach. The only time I've felt a lot of anxiety is in that first round of the best-of-five. In a seven-game series, we've always felt that the depth of our starting rotation and the depth of our pitching staff and the depth of our ball club could beat anybody. You go best-of-five and you lose one, there's a sense of urgency. You're scrambling already. One pitcher gets hot, one bad hop, one crazy thing happens and before you know it, you're scrambling. That's the only reason why the Atlanta Braves have won only one World Series. I guarantee we would have won more World Series if we were winning our division, then going straight to the NLCS. Trying to repeat is much more difficult because of this additional round. It wouldn't be as difficult in a best-of-seven because it's still going to give you a proven champion over a long period of time.

I also feel that every weekend game in the postseason should be played in the daytime. And regular season, too. I can understand playing a night game in the middle of the week. I understand why. It's because of TV and the need for prime time. But if baseball wants the kids back into the sport, it has to be available to them. There can't be games getting over at 11:30 or midnight and then the expectation for them to go to school the next day. All that is common sense. But economics and technology kind of throw a monkey wrench into it. The TV contracts are so huge. And the way the system is now, you couldn't survive without TV.

You Can't Steal First

The first three games at Coors Field went down to the wire. Maddux won 5-4, which, at Coors, is like tossing a shutout. Then we won 7-4 with Glav pitching and had to come back in the top of the ninth for four runs. In one of those games, Wohlers struck out the opposing pitcher with two outs because Colorado had run out of pinch hitters.

Those games were not decided until the ninth inning. Bobby and I were sitting there talking about what to do with the closer. You're supposed to bring your closer in if it's three runs or less; it could have been 10 runs at Colorado and we were going to bring in our closer. In the regular season, we were ahead one time 8-1 and we brought our closer in. Because 8-1 is not safe in Colorado.

We took that series three games to one and then went to Cincinnati for the NLCS. Again, we had the best record and they had home field advantage. Cincinnati was noted for its speed. In fact, we were the underdog in that series because of their team speed. The press asked me how we were going to stop Cincinnati's running game. And I looked at them and said, "Well, you can't steal first base."

See, if you make good pitches and you execute what you want to do, there is no running game because there's nobody on base. So you shift your emphasis from Cincinnati's speed to making good pitches. Once again, we're talking about the presentation, putting the staff into the mindset of negating the strength of another team. And doing it in a way that they don't know they're negating it. For example, when we're talking about making pitches, we don't tell our pitchers to slide-step from the stretch if somebody gets on base. We don't tell them that they have to move fast when they make a throw to first. None of that was ever discussed. What was discussed was how to get them out so that they wouldn't have to do any of that other stuff in the first place.

We won the first game 2-1 and the next 6-2. Both those games were extra innings, and Greg McMichael was huge in each of them. Before Wohlers took over the closer role, we had closed with Mac. He was our left-handed reliever even though he was a right-handed pitcher because of the great change-up he had. When we brought McMichael in and there was a right-hander at the plate, we wanted teams to pinch hit a left-handed hitter, because his change-up was that good.

We won the next game 5-2, and then we won 6-0 to sweep the Reds. That final game was Avery. All of a sudden the Av showed up again. We could have brought Glavine back a day early. But we knew what Avery had done in the past in big ballgames, regardless of the so-so year he'd had. You always knew that mentally he could rise to the occasion in a big game. Bobby rewarded him and, in turn, he rewarded the ball club with six shutout innings. And we basically completely shut them down. I'd like to see how many stolen bases they had that series. Four? Like I said, you can't steal first.

A BRAVE NEW WORLD

We got Cleveland in the 1995 World Series, and they were one of the great offensive teams. We were worried about Albert Belle and some of their big guns, and we finally figured out that the key to trying to beat Cleveland was to keep Kenny Lofton off the bases. He was the catalyst. Just like Dykstra was for the Phillies in '93. We shut down Lofton and everybody else. As a team, Cleveland batted .179. Lofton hit .200; Belle hit .235. That's the greatest pitching against an offensive powerhouse you can ever imagine. We shut them down completely. We completely dominated their hitters, and we did it with a lot of down and away pitches.

In the first game, Maddux was awesome, threw a two-hitter. We won the second game behind Glavine and lost the third. Av went six innings in Game 4. The change-up down and out was his main pitch. It was awesome and they just kept going after it. They didn't adjust, so he didn't have to change. I remember Steve coming into the dugout and saying, "I think they know what's coming, Leo, but they still can't hit it. Because I'm throwing so many of them."

He was going change-up, change-up, fastball, a two-to-one ratio of off-speed to fastballs. And we usually operate the opposite way. We like to work two fastballs, one off-speed. "Hey, Av," I said. "You're pitching great but you ought to mix in a few fastballs. Changing speeds is about pushing the throttle, too, just not pulling it."

He looked over at me with this look on his face, 'cause he and I would get into some arguments in the dugout. He looked at me and said, "I'm going to keep throwing it because they can't hit it."

"Okay," I said. "Sounds good to me."

"Leo, I know I'm throwing a bunch of them. But they can't hit it."

"Well, the hell with what I just said," I told him. "Just keep throwing them then."

Cleveland took Game 5 against Maddux. That's the game in which he came close to hitting Eddie Murray. He was trying to throw a cutter up and in on Murray's hands, and it sailed off toward his head a little bit. So Murray thought Maddux was throwing at him and he started yapping at Mad Dog. Charlie O'Brien was catching at the time; Charlie got in front of Eddie Murray and said, "Listen, dude, he didn't try to throw at you. That pitcher's got the greatest control of anybody in the history of the game. If he wanted to hit you, he really would've."

I rest my case there.

In Game 6, we were ahead in the series three games to two, and Omar Vizquel, Cleveland's shortstop, said in the papers, "They know they can't win a World Series." A lot of people thought the Braves couldn't win a World Series. Vizquel's comment went in one ear and out the other. I don't think he'd ever been in a World Series. So why would you even say anything like that?

Maddux told me a great thing one time. "Leo, don't ever let it get personal. Because when it gets personal, it takes away from your concentration. It'll make you try to do more than you think you can." Like I've always told the pitching staff, quietly do your job and then leave. Keep your mouth shut.

We had Glav on the mound. Maybe Cleveland had learned a lesson from Avery. After the first couple of innings, their hitters started moving up in the box and on top of the plate. Tommy came in and said, "Leo, these guys are starting to move in. They're starting to crowd me. They're starting to move in on the dish. So I guess I'd better go inside a little more, huh?"

I looked at him. "Look you've got two options," I said. "Number one, when the hitter moves up on the plate or up in the box, that doesn't change his vision. He still sees the same thing. You can go in. Or you can go out of the strike zone a littler further and see if they follow you. And if they follow you out, you're still in the same boat you were when they were off the plate. If you throw a pitch six to eight inches off the plate and there's solid contact to center field, then you have to go in more to keep the down and away open. Not necessarily to get them out, but to keep the down and away open."

Tommy's first choice was to go out a little further. They followed him out. And he still got the same results—he made them hit it on the end of the bat and get frustrated. He went inside maybe six times the entire time he was out there. It takes great control to be able to go out just a little further. That's easier said than done.

But he had great stuff that night. In the middle of the game, he came into the dugout and screamed out, "Will somebody please score a damned run? Because they're not."

So Dave Justice comes up in the sixth inning and we're at home at the Chop Shop. It was the Indians' first World Series in decades, and their fans back in Cleveland were fired up. It was loud at Jacobs Field. Which made the Chop Shop seem not so loud. Justice had made a comment about it in the local papers, and some of the fans were on him. As a coach I try not to pay attention to all that. But there's definitely a difference when there's a packed house. There's more excitement. You pitch better, you hit better, you coach better, everybody's more alert. I think atmosphere does elevate play. And David wanted to see a little more hoorah. When we went into Pittsburgh in the early '90s and they didn't sell out, we'd say, gee, look at these empty seats. We never thought we'd see that at home. But Justice fired them up that night; he hit a solo home run that put us ahead 1-0. It was the only run that Glavine would need.

My concerns at that point were two: when would the fatigue factor set in with Glavine? And could he get us to Wohlers in the ninth? Or pitch the ninth himself? After eight, Glav was one bloop single shy of a no-hitter. He was nailing the down and away strike automatically. He had made the adjustment we'd discussed earlier in the game, and the Cleveland hitters didn't adjust.

We had to make the decision: leave Glavine in or bring in Wohlers? There are a couple of times I remember over the years when there were difficult decisions for Bobby to make. One was when Avery had a 1-0 lead in Pittsburgh; we took him out after eight. The other was Glavine pitching in the 1-0 game against Cleveland. Both pitchers came to us and said they were tired. So the decision Bobby had to make was whether to start a tired pitcher out there in the ninth inning and hope that he gets through it, or bring in a fresh pitcher. You had Mark Wohlers. Come on. Mark Wohlers was tremendous that year. And in the Avery game in Pittsburgh, you had Alejandro Pena. So it's basically common sense.

Let me tell you something: Wohlers comes in and Kenny Lofton's leading off. And you know if he gets Lofton out, we're going to win the World Series. That's the key to that whole inning. We know if Lofton gets on, we'll be in trouble because Wohlers can't hold runners. We know that if Lofton gets on, he's going to steal second and possibly steal third. The only way we could keep them from scoring was for Wohlers to strike out the side with somebody on base. Which Mark was very capable of doing. But why go through that?

Wohlers didn't like throwing over to first base. I don't know how it developed, but he had a thing about throwing to first. We got to a point where we just didn't want him to throw over there any more because he simply couldn't make the throw. We always felt that more teams should have known about it, but they didn't.

With Mark not being able to throw over to first base, as a coach once again you get back to de-emphasizing the problem. We worked on throwing quick to the plate, but he wasn't real comfortable with that either. I decided that you just had to show that you had it, so he would slide-step to the plate periodically. And once you planted the seed, that at least would give them something to think about.

There's no way I would have taken him out and told him, "Let's practice throwing over to first." Because I knew that the physical part of that had nothing to do with it—you can practice it all you want. Like Johnny Sain told me, you go into another area to get their mind off the problem. And before you know it, the problem's not as big any more. We had all these teams checking us out and following us all through the year, and nobody figured out that we couldn't throw over to first base. I don't know what in the hell they were looking at.

So we knew that was the key, getting Lofton out in the ninth inning, and when Lofton popped up to third in foul territory, I knew that we had it.

After the last out, I just sat there. I don't go between the lines. I feel that's for the players. A coach should be in the background. It's just something I believe in. I don't go out there and physically perform, so I don't go between the white lines. But that moment was great. I didn't scream, I didn't holler. It was kind of a load off. It was a lot of quiet satisfaction. We celebrated with champagne and all. The moment it happened, people were running all over the place. It's hard to believe; I was kind of calm.

FIFTH INNING:

THE HOUSE THAT RUTH BUILT

John Smoltz had his breakthrough season in 1996. He finished 24-8 with an ERA of 2.94 and won the Cy Young Award. Smoltzie jumped out hot and never stopped. At one point, he had a 14-game win streak. He had a tremendous year. Well, he has a tremendous year every year; it's just that the numbers fell into place. Glavine's ERA was 2.98 that year and he was 15-11. Maddux was 2.72 and 15-11. Somebody might say they had an off year. They didn't. There are a lot of things that determine a win-loss record. Sometimes, you get a lot of no-decisions, or you have a lot of close and low-scoring losses. And look at the innings pitched. Smoltz led the league, Maddux was second, and Glavine fifth.

Did you know John Smoltz won 29 games in 1996? He won 24 regular-season games, he won four starts in the postseason, and he won the All-Star game. He was almost a

30-game winner that year. He just dominated the National League. At times, he had just overpowering performances.

John pitched a game against Cincinnati, and he started off with 26 straight fastballs. Unheard of. Bobby looks up and said, "Well, I guess this is fastball night tonight, huh, Leo? Where the hell is the breaking ball?"

Smoltzie came in and I asked him whether he was going to mix in any breaking balls. He told me they were sitting on the breaking balls, looking for them, so he was throwing all fastballs. Then once he gave up a hit, he started mixing it up. He told me he was setting them up for the next time he faced them because now they were going to be looking for all fastballs and he was going to throw all sliders.

That was the year Andruw Jones arrived in Atlanta. He was 19 years old and made the jump from Single-A ball to the major leagues in two months. That's unheard of.

He's the greatest center fielder I've ever seen. If you're going to compare him to somebody, you've got to compare him to the great Willie Mays. And he had that as a rookie. Marquis Grissom was our center fielder, so Bobby played Andruw mostly in right field that year. Everybody saw the raw talent. Especially the pitchers. Greg Maddux would come up to me and whisper in my ear, "Can you tell Bobby to put that guy in center field when I'm pitching?"

And that's just what Bobby did.

THE COMEBACK

We finished eight games above Montreal in the Eastern Division and had to meet the Dodgers in the first round. L.A.

is a tough place to play because you're out on the West Coast and everything's so nice out there. We pitched our butts off against the Dodgers. We swept them, but they were all low-scoring games. The most runs they scored in any game was two. The first game went 10 innings. You know, what's new? It seems like we always get into these 10-inning things.

Then we faced the Cardinals in the NLCS. St. Louis is a great baseball town. It's fun, but it's a tough place to win. Just like Dodger Stadium. There are certain places where the intensity level is higher, as opposed to going into a stadium like Montreal where you really have to get yourself up. You go to those places like St. Louis and Los Angeles, you're up. The stadiums get you up. The atmosphere.

We went down to the Cardinals three games to one. Boy, do I remember that. Smoltz pitched a beautiful game in Game 1; then we lost Games 2 and 3 and 4. We got a heckuva wake-up call. They thought the playoffs were over. They were staring at our dugout and all that stuff; good old Dennis Eckersley was pumping his fist. It certainly didn't hurt our cause. Believe me, our ballplayers saw that and nobody had to say a word. Not a word. Because 3-1 doesn't mean the thing's over. We went out and smoked them the very next day in Busch Stadium, 14-0. It gets back to the theory we believe in: quietly win, quietly get the job done, and leave. We came back to Atlanta. Maddux pitched a six-hitter, and then Glavine pitched a four-hit shutout.

And now it's back to the World Series. Our fourth in the last five. Only this time, we're defending champions. And we're going to Yankee Stadium. Now, you want to talk about the ultimate? *That* is the ultimate. You want to talk about a bigger thrill than the last pitch of the '95 World Series? The first pitch of the '96 World Series.

You get to Yankee Stadium and on the big screen are pictures of Mickey Mantle and all the great Yankees. Joe DiMaggio throws out the first ball. There's the public address announcer, Bob Sheppard, whom I grew up listening to: "And now playing center field, number 7, Mickey Mantle. Number 7." He had his own unique way of announcing. And I couldn't wait until they said, "Leo Mazzone, number 54, pitching coach, the Atlanta Braves."

We'd be down in the bullpen before the games and those fans would be going crazy. Calling out, "Hey, Leo! You should be up here. You're Italian and should be in New York." I threw up a couple of balls and somebody said, "Hey, Mazzone! Where's my ball?" When I hollered back that we had to save the rest for the game, they made reference to my Italian heritage. And in a not very flattering way. But you enjoy it if you play along with them. If you show them they're getting to you, you can forget about it.

Yankee Stadium has such a mystique: the clubhouse, the monuments, the facade. Whitey Ford pitched there—my idol. You walk in through the tunnels under Yankee Stadium knowing that all those legends have walked under there. Even the building you see behind the right center field wall in Yankee Stadium. I don't even know what that building is, but I remember seeing it as a kid. The people are there in the Bronx and they're ready to roll. It's just awesome.

I'll never forget going down to the bullpen in left center field. In Yankee Stadium, both teams reach the bullpens through the same entrance. I'm walking down before the first game with Smoltzie. And Mel Stottlemyre, their pitching coach, is walking down with Andy Pettitte. There are some pitching coaches who don't speak to you. For example, in St. Louis nobody will speak to you; some people like to walk around with their nose in the air. My starting pitcher was running a few sprints to warm up his legs and his starter was, too. So Mel and I started shooting the bull in front of 60,000 some-odd going crazy in Yankee Stadium.

"Hey, Mel," I said. "How does Andy Petite cut that dang slider down on right-handed hitters' feet? How does he throw that pitch?"

He looks at me and goes, "Leo, I'll tell you how to throw that pitch if you tell me how Maddux throws his cutter."

"Well," I said, "you go first."

Guess what? Mel went first and told me that Andy Petite threw his hard breaking ball with a stiff wrist. I teach a loose wrist. I told Stottlemyre that Maddux brings that hard cutter off his index finger, not his middle finger. "Well, that's interesting," he said. "I'm going to try that."

"Yeah, I'm going to try yours, too," I said.

THE GREATEST HEARTBREAK

In '96, I thought we were better than the Yankees. In '99, when they swept us in the World Series, I did not think we were better than the Yankees. But in '96, we had the package, man. We went to Yankee Stadium and kicked their butts the first two games of the Series and didn't win another game. Which is amazing to me.

The first two games, it was all Braves. Smoltz won 12-1 on a four-hitter. Maddux came back in Game 2 and won 4-0. It was another Maddux gem, and Smoltzie was great. Andruw

Jones came up and slammed two home runs right out of the gate, and I was thinking, wow!

We lost Game 3, 5-3. They scored three in the eighth. Tommy pitched a great game. If the score is 2-1 going into the eighth, you know your starting pitcher's done a helluva job.

Game 4 in Atlanta is the one everyone remembers, the three-run homer that Mark Wohlers gave up to Jim Leyritz on a hanging slider to tie the game. We were up two games to one in the Series and rolling. We had a 6-0 lead going into the sixth inning. Denny Neagle, who had come over late in the year from Pittsburgh, started the game and was pitching great.

There's no way you can blame Wohlers for that home run to Leyeritz. If you're going to look at anything, and this is nothing against Denny Neagle, but if you go into the sixth inning with a six-run lead and can't get out of the sixth inning … that's what started the whole thing. That made us use Wohlers in the eighth inning instead of the ninth, because we were trying to protect a lead and there was a sense of urgency. And Mark hung a slider that he intended to throw in the dirt.

After Mark gave up that home run to Leyritz, he came into the dugout and I looked at him and I said, "Don't ever second-guess yourself. Because if you'd thrown that slider in the dirt where you wanted it, he'd have missed it by three feet. You didn't try to leave it up on purpose."

Here's the scenerio you run into with pitchers like Mark Wohlers or John Rocker. They both throw close to 100 mph. If they get their fastballs hit, somebody is going to say, "Well, he needs to throw some more breaking balls; he needs to mix things up." Then if they throw some breaking balls and a breaking ball gets hit, they're going to say, "How in the hell can he let them hit a breaking ball when he throws it a hundred miles an hour?"

As a coach, you know that you always have to complement one pitch with another. We know it isn't the pitch you selected. Whatever you selected, if it ended up where you wanted it to, you never give up a hit. That eliminates second-guessing.

Wohlers is not the reason we lost that World Series. It was very important to say that to him. Who do you think feels worse having given up that home run? Mark Wohlers. Mark Wohlers is a pitcher who has shown me more courage than any other pitcher I've ever coached because of what he's gone through since, and he had the guts to go out there and continue on. There are a lot of guys who would have cashed in their chips. Therefore, you don't second-guess the young man for leaving the slider up. I know he wanted to throw a slider in the dirt for a swing and a miss. I think he made the right choice, regardless of the end result.

Avery came in to pitch in the 10th inning with two guys on base and the score tied. He intentionally walked Bernie Williams to load the bases and get to Wade Boggs. We thought Avery was a great matchup with Boggs. Lefty to lefty. When you have a change-up that dies like Avery's did, left-handers don't see that kind of pitch too much. It was a huge weapon. Avery was up 1-2 in the count and lost it. It's Wade Boggs at bat, and it ain't easy getting a called strike on Wade Boggs. Those pitches were close. I've never looked at the film to see how close, but they were close. It wasn't like Avery was wild. Boggs fought off some pitches and laid off some other pitches that might have been an inch off the plate. But we liked that matchup. I don't know how many pitches he threw to him in that sequence.

The fifth game was the classic 1-0, Smoltz vs. Petitte. Smoltzie pitched eight innings. And then he told me he was done. "If there's a Game 7, Leo, don't ask me to pitch in relief," he said. "I won't be able to pick up a baseball again until spring training." That's how fatigued he was.

The only run of the game scored after Jermaine Dye, in right field, ran in front of Marquis Grissom on a fly ball, and Grissom dropped the ball. That was the only run that scored in the whole damn game. The game ended when we pinch hit Luis Polonia and he hit that ball into right center with runners on first and third. Paul O'Neil ran it down.

Game 6 was back in Yankee Stadium, Maddux against Jimmy Key. He pitched a great game. He shut down all the Yankee batters except for the catcher. He left a pitch to Joe Girardi—who had caught Mad Dog in Chicago—up over the plate, and Girardi hit a triple to put them ahead 3-2. Maddux came in the dugout in the sixth. He said, "I'm getting tired."

"I don't care," I said. "You can't get tired."

"I'm telling you, I'm running out of gas."

"I don't give a shit," I said. "Reach down into your bag of tricks. All you've got to do is get three more outs. Then we'll pull out the win."

He said, "That's what I'm trying to tell you; this bag's empty."

So I went to Bobby and said, "Bobby, Mad Dog says he's tired."

Bobby didn't skip a beat. "Tell him he can't be."

Mad Dog went out and got the side out.

It was difficult when we made the last out in the World Series. We had runners at first and second and popped up to third base. John Wetteland was closing, and it always seemed like we had a runner or two on base. That was a downer, losing that last game in Yankee Stadium. Losing that World Series was tough because of the way we started off.

From the final three games of NLCS through the first two games of the World Series, the Braves scored 48 runs and gave up only two. That is incredible. What tremendous pitching. Two runs in five games in the postseason?

The final games in four of our World Series were decided by one run. We lost three World Series by three runs. In 1991, the final game was 1-0. In 1992, the final game was 4-3. In 1995, we won the final game 1-0. And in 1996, we lost the final game 1-0. You've got four one-run games deciding the World Series. That's about as close as it gets. And I don't apologize to anyone.

We had a great team in 1996. That one, we should have won.

THANKS FOR THE MEMORIES

That was our last season at Atlanta Fulton-County Stadium, the Chop Shop. I have fond memories there. My fondest is something somebody said, how we had destroyed the myth of the Launching Pad. That's first and foremost in my mind. And then the tomahawk chop and the intimidation factor we had as a result of our home field from '91 to '96. It was loud and it was exciting. It was energized and it was electric.

The Launching Pad turned out to be one of the more pitcher-friendly parks compared to the ones that are being built now and what has evolved offensively in baseball since 1996. Everybody used to love to go there and hit. And that's just more testament to the great pitching that took place from 1991 to 1996 in Atlanta-Fulton County Stadium.

Turner Field is a beautiful stadium. I think it's the most beautiful of all the new ballparks. The dimensions at Turner Field are the same as the Chop Shop. But it's an open stadium. Atlanta-Fulton County was enclosed like a pancake, and you had wind swirls. There were tunnels down both lines, and if you hit it that way, the wind through the tunnels would just rocket the ball out of there.

I think Turner Field is a park that's fair to pitchers and hitters. You may have some arguments from hitting instructors. But these days, the way some parks are, it's more than fair. And gorgeous.

I watched them implode the Chop Shop on TV. And it brought back some tremendous memories. Probably the top one was Cabrera driving in Sid Bream. There was the three-game series against the Dodgers in '91. The pennant races ... all the excitement. It was a joint that was hopping. It was jumping. It was like the old Boston Garden used to be. There was a game Smoltzie was pitching against the Dodgers in '91. It was during a three-game series in September. He gave up a run or two in the first inning and came in and said, "You can't believe how loud it is out there. It's throwing my equilibrium off."

"You'd better get used to it," I said. "Because that's all you're going to hear from here on out." I mean, you could feel the dugout shake.

And I remember the gigantic home runs. I remember Jack Clark hit one off Tommy Glavine, one of the longest ones I've ever seen. Another thing that made Atlanta-Fulton County Stadium such a good ballpark was the grounds crew. The playing surface ended up being good. You add a range of good infielders and a good playing surface to a good pitching staff, and that certainly helped destroy the myth of the Launch Pad.

A Trip to the Mound ...

Every season is long, and there are the occasional flareups with the pitchers you're coaching. And there are moments that can get very profane. We were in Colorado one time; Avery was pitching and getting his butt kicked. Then he hit Galarraga. I don't think he did it on purpose. He was just over-throwing because he was upset. So I went out to the mound and when I got there, he said, "What the fuck are you doing out here?"

That really shocked me. I'd never had a pitcher say that to me. And so I looked at him and I thought for a second and said, "Well, now that you've asked me, I'm out here to tell you to go fuck yourself. How do you like that?"

And he said, "Well, now that you've told me, are you gonna leave?"

I said, "No, I have one more thing to add. Go fuck yourself, you fucking asshole! Now I'm gonna leave." I turned around and walked back in the dugout.

I got back to the dugout and Bobby knew something had happened. "Hey, is everything all right out there?" he asked.

"Everything's fine," I said.

The next day, the pitching coach for San Diego, came over and said, "On behalf of the rest of the major leagues, we'd like to thank you for your display out on the mound yesterday."

Of course, Av apologized. Smoltzie, Mad Dog and Glavine were having fun with it. They were in there watching it on TV. "Oh watch this; Leo's gonna go nuts!"

It was no big deal. "That's all right, Av," I told him. "Just don't do it again. When I come out to the mound, you don't have to listen. But you respect what I'm trying to do. And I'll respect what you're trying to do."

There was a big blow-up with Glavine one time. Tommy was getting beat in St. Louis, and they were hitting some shots off him. Then they dinked one in on the right field line. And he came into the dugout and yelled out, "They're blooping me to death!"

"That's not what I'm seeing," I told him. "I'm seeing balls wrapping off those walls out there. What are you seeing? And you're throwing all these sliders, which we never do. What are you trying to do? Reinvent the wheel out there?"

"You're always pushing me, Leo," he said. "You're always pushing me."

"Yeah," I said. "That's the way I coach."

So he got angry. He was standing by the runway, threw his glove at me and called me some names and went up the runway. I picked up the glove, called him the same names, and threw it back at him.

Bobby was standing there like the stoic figure that he is, that glove flying by his ear. Twice. We ended up winning the game. It was one of the very few games that Glav didn't pitch real well. When we came into the clubhouse, everybody shakes hands. So I shook Tommy's hand and he gave me kind of a begrudging thanks.

As soon as we did that, Avery and Merker came hustling over and, in these falsetto voices, said to me, "You gave in first, you gave in first. We saw that; you extended your hand first. You gave in."

Everybody was laughing. I sat down in front of my locker. Maddux had done the chart that night. He had on his little Peabody glasses and he came over. "Hey, Coach?" he asked in this really innocent voice. "What happened out there with you and Glavine? You guys get into a fight or something?"

"No," I said. "Just coach and pitcher hollering at each other."

"Well," Maddux said. "You must have really upset Tommy because he came in here and destroyed the clubhouse and called you a no-good SOB. I don't know if I should tell you that or not." I looked up at him and he said nothing for a moment. "You know, I don't know if I should tell you this either," he said. "But he called you a fat, balding rotund piece of crap. But I don't know if I should tell you that or not."

I finally told him to give me that chart before I put it someplace where the sun don't shine.

You're going to have your things like that. Greg McMichael was a great kid, and I was trying to get a point across to him early in his career. He asked me to stop and said, "I don't mind you getting on me, Leo, but I don't appreciate the language you're using."

"I'm sorry, Mac, I didn't know you didn't like that," I said. "So let me put it to you another way." And then I eliminated the cuss words. So there's always adjustments being made.

But it's all in good fun. And over the years, a lot of respect has developed for all concerned.

You try to make everybody feel wanted and feel like they belong. That doesn't mean there's not constructive criticism. Or that you don't deal with someone who doesn't want to put in the time or the preparation. But I've never gotten upset with a pitcher if he got beat. The only thing I get upset with is the lack of preparation, the lack of dedication, not giving it any thought or thinking it ought to be handed to them on a platter without earning it.

Sometimes you have to sit them down and talk about it. Beforehand, you determine what type of approach you're going to take and what kind of language you're going to use. How loud you're going to be or how quiet you're going to be. You have to discuss it with the individual according to their personality. Then you play it by ear and hope somebody doesn't clock you.

That's almost happened a couple of times. You hope your power as coach works because you know there's no way in hell you can physically take these guys. I had one guy in the minor leagues, he could tear a phone book in two. We were in Double A and he was angry because he wasn't in Triple A. He'd take it out on his teammates. He would be at the ballpark complaining every day. Then one day he punched out another pitcher.

I said, "If you're such a tough guy, let's go into the clubhouse and into this little room here."

He said, "Yeah, let's go."

So I take him down there and all I'm thinking is: oh, golly, I'm about to get *killed*. I took him into the room and said, "You know, you wake up in the morning, look in the mirror and you get angry. 'Cause you don't like it here."

"I shouldn't be here," he said.

"Maybe so," I said. "But you *are* here and we're trying to make the best of it. You're a strong son of a gun, aren't you? You can kick anybody's butt on the team."

"I sure can," he said.

"I want you to show me how tough you really are," I said. "I want you to get on the phone and call Hank Aaron. Tell him how upset you are and how you don't like it here. Hank's a good friend of mine, so I'll tell him it's okay that you called. You're a tough guy. You call him and tell him how you don't like it here. You don't like the manager, you don't like being in Double A. Show me how tough you are."

Thank God the point I was trying to get across to him sank in. Because the guy could have killed me.

There are managers who don't like pitchers. The pitchers are their excuses for not winning, and so they don't handle them right. There used to be the ones who would holler at pitchers and cuss at them. Or carry on like a nut in the dugout. Those days are gone. By the same token, that doesn't mean you're not firm or get your point across in a different way. It's hard to hide facial expressions sometimes. But there are going to be times when I want a pitcher to see my facial expressions. Ultimately, it's the manager taking care of the pitching staff, and how he handles it determines how easy or difficult my job is going to be. Believe me, when you're with Bobby, the job's not difficult.

I was working with big Marvin Freeman one time, and he just came out and told me, "I don't want to do it this way."

In that situation, you have to stand firm. I said, "If you don't want to do it this way, why don't you pack your bags and leave?"

He goes, "What do you mean?"

"You have so much to offer," I said. "But you keep breaking down physically. If you would just trust me on what I tell you and not try to intimidate me because you're six foot eight and I'm five-nine. That's not going to work. Besides, see number 6 in there? The manager? He backs me a hundred percent." And that was the end of that.

Of course, you have your fun moments, too. One time Mad Dog gave up some runs and he was getting all over me. He came in all upset and said, "Tell me something different, Leo. Don't give me the usual clichés."

"Okay," I said. "Well, fuck you then!"

He gave me this hurt look. "What'd you tell me *that* for?"

"Well," I said. "You told me to tell you something different. I haven't told you *that* in eight years."

Then I grinned and Mad Dog started picking at his spikes. "Hey, good comeback, Coach."

SIXTH INNING:
THE BEST FIVESOME

S teve Avery left after the 1996 season and signed with the Boston Red Sox. Basically, it was like losing a son. I saw Avery at a reunion a little while later and he said, "You don't have anybody to cuss at any more. They're all good guys now; there's nobody to cuss out."

Avery meant so much to the Atlanta Braves and to all of us through the years. He was a great pitcher, a great kid, the best young pitcher I ever had the privilege of coaching. Winning 18 games when he was 21 years old. And then the huge games he pitched in the postseason. He was a tremendous competitor, great stuff. He was the Dodger killer, the baby-faced killer. I see him today and he still looks like a kid, doesn't even look like he shaves. Arm troubles eventually forced him to retire. You hate to see that happen.

Kevin Millwood was called up in the middle of 1997. And I remember he pitched a great game in Boston, going seven innings in a 15-2 win. What we loved about Millwood was that he wasn't intimidated by the standard of excellence we'd set in Atlanta. He wasn't intimidated by who was on the pitching staff. He picked their brains. He had a good work ethic. He was a country boy who didn't say much, just let his pitching do his talking. It was great to have that addition to the staff.

I remember a game he pitched against the Cubs. Mark Grace came up to me and said, "How do you guys do this? You bring somebody up and this guy is *dealing*."

I never taught Avery a pitch. With Millwood, it was always trying to keep him from getting too long in his mechanics and kind of lumbering around a little bit. He was an attacker; he'd attack with his fastball. It was a heavy ball. His mound presence, from the get-go, was real good. You can look at a pitcher's mound presence and know a lot of times how much confidence he has in his ability to win. In Millwood's case, he had the mound presence. We always thought that Millwood, in his first year, looked like a veteran.

We had four starters in 1997 in the top 10 ERA leaders. You hope for a couple. That was a great foursome. I always thought that Glavine, Maddux, Smoltz and Avery were the top foursome. Then I felt Glavine, Maddux, Smoltz and Denny Neagle were the top foursome. The top fivesome came the next season with the emergence of Millwood.

Greg Maddux was Greg Maddux in 1997, just his usual self with great control and great movement. He finished 19-4 with a 2.20 ERA. Even after having worked with him all those years, I'm still amazed at his ability to hit a target. He walked 20 people all year, and six of those were intentional. So that means 14 walks over the course of an entire season. That's unbelievable, period. That's a testament to great control and great movement. And to his greatness. It's Hall of Fame stuff. And it's something Atlanta's been privileged to witness over a period of time. They'll appreciate it even more when he's not here any more.

Glavine's year is the perfect example of how a record can be deceiving. He finished 14-7. But his ERA was 2.96, lower than Denny Neagle, who won 20 games. Tommy had 12 no-decisions that year, and most of those were decided by one run. He was fifth in the league in innings pitched, and, like I said, that's the statistic I consider most important.

We got Neagle, a left-hander, from Pittsburgh late in the '96 season. He fit in right away. He fit in great. We traded a great young prospect for him, Jason Schmidt. That's actually the best thing that could have happened to Jason, because he got the opportunity to pitch every five days for Pittsburgh, and he was able to develop and continue his career with San Francisco.

Neagle was a funny dude. He was a prankster for four days. On the fifth day when he pitched, you couldn't talk to him. He'd come in with the look on his face. With Glavine, you can't tell if he's pitching or not. Same with Maddux. With Smoltzie, he had a little more bounce in his step on the day he was pitching. Avery just pulled his hat down and went to work.

His stuff was borderline, as far as pure stuff. He had a fastball and change-up. Denny pitched in quads. What I mean by quads is down and away, up and away, down and in, up and in. Denny threw more breaking balls than Tommy Glavine threw in the course of a nine-inning game. But we got him to start throwing the ball down and away to set up everything else, which helped make him a 20-game winner.

He was the only pitcher in the National League to win 20 in 1997. He could have won more; he might have won the Cy Young. It would have taken 22 or 23 wins because Pedro Martinez was having a great year in Montreal, but he could have done it if he hadn't hurt his right shoulder. He'd just finished a side session with me and he was throwing great. He loved throwing all the time in between starts and became a top-shelf starter. He was good when we got him, but he got better when he was here.

I got into the clubhouse and Bobby said, "Hey, Neagle's hurt."

"He can't be," I said. "I just had him throw in the bullpen, and he threw great."

"He did something out in the outfield," Bobby said.

Denny hurt his shoulder in right field after our session. He dove for a ball, or something silly like that, and hurt his right, non-throwing, shoulder. Neagle was scared to death to come and tell me because he knew what my reaction was going to be. He was correct. I really got on him. "What in the hell is wrong with you? Are you crazy?"

As a pitching coach, your main goal is the health of your pitching staff so that they have the opportunity to go out and perform. If you go to the post when it's your turn, the rest will take care of itself. If you get hurt during a game, you can understand that. But not horsing around in the outfield.

That was the year Andruw Jones became our regular center fielder. Believe me, when Andruw Jones took over in center, our staff ERA was measurably helped by that. A lot of opposing coaches and managers have said to me, "Have you ever told your pitchers that they all need to go out and get Andruw Jones a Mercedes for what he means to the pitching staff out there in center field?" You don't really realize what he means until you look one day and he's not out there because he's taking one of his rare days off. When someone hits one to the gap and it falls, you go, "What happened there?" And what happened was that a normal center fielder couldn't get to that ball, but Andruw Jones would have run it down.

We started off hot that year, winning 12 of our first 13. We finished with 101 wins, nine games ahead of Florida in our division. It was the most wins in the National League and our sixth straight division title.

We had Houston in the division series and swept them. We were kind of in Houston's head. Maddux won 2-1 at Turner Field. He beat Darryl Kile, and Kile gave up only one hit. He pitched a one-hitter and Maddux beat him. In a best-of-five, that was huge. Glavine won Game 2 13-3. And Smoltzie closed it out with a 4-1 win in the Astrodome. We had great battles with Houston. They always had good pitching. They always seemed to be close games. The atmosphere in the Dome was good. It was loud. But once again, you're in a first-round best-of-five and you're pulling out whatever hair you have remaining.

THE WIDEST STRIKE ZONE

We played the wild card team, the Florida Marlins, in the NLCS. They were loaded that year: Kevin Brown, Moises

Alou, Gary Sheffield and Bobby Bonilla. Maddux pitched the first game and lost 5-3, all five runs unearned. When Maddux does lose, it's because of bloop hits or errors. Very seldom does he go out there and just get his butt kicked. Maddux and Kevin Brown was a great matchup. Kevin Brown is one of the better pitchers we've played against over the years.

Tommy won the second game 7-1. He came up big. I can't really remember any of our starting pitchers not coming up big in the postseason. Every once in a while you might get an early KO, but they were few and far between considering the number of games we've played.

We split the next two games, and then came the turning point, Game 5, Maddux against Livan Hernandez. We lost, 2-1. That game was a joke. It was the widest strike zone I've ever seen. Chipper Jones and Freddie McGriff came back to the dugout after striking out on those back-door breaking balls that were way outside. They just said, "We can't hit that pitch, we can't *reach* it." The other teams always moan about the strike zone that Braves pitchers have, but our pitchers have great control. And Livan Hernandez had great control that day. If he knows he's getting calls that far off the plate, he's still got to be able to throw it there. And he did it on a consistent basis.

We always felt that if an umpire had a liberal strike zone, we could use it to our advantage. But that one, basically, was ridiculous. Hernandez had 15 strikeouts, and he's not a strike-out pitcher. We lost, 2-1.

That was the year Florida had gone out to get some good ballplayers. They had a darned good club. It's a damned shame what happened to them after that season. They got picked apart, and that was a slap in the face to the fans. You finally get a winner, it lasts one year and then you're done. Which is another testament to what the Braves have accomplished over a 12-year span.

They had a good ball club, but that series kind of left a sour taste in my mouth. We'd won the division over Florida by nine games. And then we didn't get back to the World Series after being in it two years in a row in '95 and '96. We wanted another crack at the Yankees. But the Yankees ended up losing, too. And it was Florida against Cleveland.

We didn't play well in certain facets of the game in that series, especially defensively. Which was very unusual for us, because defense has always been one of our strong suits. That was a very empty feeling, getting beat by Florida. But they went on to become world champions, so they were doing something right.

THE BEST FIVESOME

John Smoltz had elbow surgery in the off season and started 1998 on the disabled list. He had to live with that the whole season. But John was able to pitch through it and pitch extremely effectively. He was 17-3 and led the league in winning percentage. So when his elbow was okay, he was, too. And there were a lot of times he pitched when he wasn't okay. That's just Smoltzie. He could go out there and power his way through; he could go out there and finesse his way through. We already know he's got the greatest breaking ball of any right-hander I've ever coached. Smoltzie has a knack of being able to compete, and he did it that year without being a hundred percent.

We won 106 games that year, a franchise record and the sixth most wins in National League history. We led the major leagues in ERA, shutouts and strikeouts. We had five starters who won at least 16 games. That's happened only once in the history of the major leagues—the Pittsburgh Pirates did it in 1902. Tommy Glavine won the Cy Young for a second time. Mad Dog won the ERA title.

People talk about which foursome was the best; that was the best fivesome. The reason we could win 106 games was that we had a huge advantage after you got past the number three starter. Our four and five holes were as good as the one and two holes on a lot of teams. You don't get into losing streaks when you're running five guys like that out there. You come to the ballpark feeling pretty confident and pretty good.

Tommy won the Cy Young in 1991, then won it again in 1998. To win 20 games in this era is very difficult because you only have 35 starts a year. Used to be, you'd have 40-plus starts because of the four-man rotations. Even though Tommy won the Cy Young, there were years when he pitched just as well and didn't win the Cy Young. The same goes for Maddux.

Yeah, that was a great five: Glavine, Maddux, Smoltz, Neagle and Millwood. The greatest starting five since 1902. In thinking back, it's amazing what they accomplished. All five were at the top of their game. You run them out every night. We could get into a lot of team's heads. They'd go: Who's starting today? Who's starting tomorrow? Oh, brother, there's no breather.

WILD PITCH

In a three-year span, Mark Wohlers had become one of the elite closers in the game. In those three years, he saved 97 games. He was pretty much automatic, but there always was concern. He had developed that little throwing tic going to first base. Bobby and I always sat in the dugout and said, "Let's hope someday it never carries over to sixty feet, six inches."

He pitched a long time with a few little tics, and he was still saving games. And you also thought that if he got a little wild, there wasn't anything wrong with that because the hitters would be scared to death. So we were trying to use all these positives. We'd say, "Just think if one gets away and you nearly floor somebody, they're gonna want no part of you." Not that we wanted him to do that, but we were trying to give him all the positives we could to help him break out of it.

He started out wild in spring training and then kind of broke out of it at the start of the year. Then it just went south on him. That was tough. He was very hard on himself. He'd be down in the bullpen trying to practice his control and he'd be cussing himself out, calling himself names. I did everything I could to put the thought process on mechanics, but we all knew it was mental. Here's what it is: a fear of going out and embarrassing yourself by losing control of your pitches.

That's what happened to Steve Blass of Pittsburgh; he had great control and then he suddenly couldn't throw a strike. It's a mental thing. In the baseball world, they call it "The Monkey." Where you get a monkey on your back. Once you get that, it never goes away. But there are gorillas and then are spider monkeys.

The courage that Mark displayed by continuing to practice, continuing to go out there and try to get it done, was tremendous. A lot of guys would have just shut it down for a while, just to give their brain a rest. And he didn't do that.

It's very frustrating for a coach, but nowhere near as frustrating as it is for the individual. I went through the same kind of thing throwing batting practice. I reached a point where I had trouble throwing strikes when I used to be a machine doing that. So I could relate to what was going on. You start trying different grips and different pressures and experimenting like a son of a gun. Before you know it, you've forgotten how to throw the ball in the first place. But can you imagine trying to get through it on national TV in front of a packed house at the stadium? That's why he's so courageous, not being afraid to go out there and try.

My approach to him sure as hell wasn't hollering and screaming and carrying on. That's for darn sure. It was just to continue to give him support and to downplay it. Sometimes he felt pretty good with his slider, so he'd throw all sliders. We were hoping he'd find positives to build on. Every so often, he'd show signs of breaking out of it. And you'd say, "Okay, man, here we go!"

It was very difficult. No coach can figure those things out. I don't care who you are. If somebody said it was his mechanics, that's a bunch of BS. Because your mental approach affects your mechanics.

He was eventually put on the disabled list, and they listed it "unable to pitch." It was very tough to put him on the DL because of the type of person that Mark is. He's a great kid. It was very tough to try to understand the emotions he was going through.

Baseball is a cruel business. I've seen people get on other people about being wild, making fun of it. I always remind them: we don't need that crap, people have feelings. Whether it's the opposition or somebody from within trying to be funny, that ain't funny. It's not like he's trying to do it. In fact, he's trying so hard *not* to do it that it escalates the problem. And nobody can figure that out. I don't care who you are. That has to be an individual thing that they figure out for themselves.

It was sad. He ended up practicing so hard and trying to get his control right that it's probably how he tore his elbow up when he went to Cincinnati in '99. You couldn't talk him into stopping. You pretty much had to let him try to work things out. That was a difficult time. He's recovered from it now to the degree that he's pitching again. But he's not the same guy he was when he dominated the National League.

When we lost Wohlers, Kerry Ligtenberg and John Rocker and Mike Cather did a great job for us. Rocker set up, Cather set up and Kerry closed. He saved 30 games. We found him pitching in Minnesota in the independent league for a team that our old catcher, Greg Olson, owned. We gave six dozen baseballs and two dozen bats to Greg Olson when we signed Ligtenberg.

Bill Fisher was the Triple-A pitching coach in Richmond who worked with them, and he sent us up three guys who took the ball and ran with it. Rocker did a good job as the setup guy, and Cather was good. And Light would come in, one of the coolest and calmest guys I ever saw out there, closing games with no experience. You couldn't tell whether he was closing or just pitching the middle of an inning. I kept thinking: I hope you don't wake up and realize where you are. He was a very cool customer, one of the finest individuals I've ever met. Fish did a great job with those three recommendations, that's for sure.

We also picked up Rudy Seanez in 1998, and he pitched great for us. He's another pitcher who's never done anything anywhere else. But when he was with us, he did a tremendous job. Rudy developed a change-up that allowed him to be successful, much like the one that Mike Remlinger would develop. All the scouts were calling it a split, but it was a change-up thrown hard. An effective change-up is the least amount you can take off and still make it work. Because it promotes everything on the pitch you're looking for—action on the pitch, location, arm speed and deception, so that you're not giving anything away. I've seen Remlinger throw change-ups at 83, 84 mph. Rudy, too. But their fastballs are 91, 92. Rudy did a great job for us; he just couldn't stay healthy.

Maddux pitched a game against the Blue Jays in June that lasted 1:46, the shortest game in the major leagues since 1992. A 2-0 win. Well under two hours. It went something like this: strike one, strike two, strike three. Or strike one, you're out. The thing with Mad Dog is the batter has to decide whether he's going to attack him or wait him out. If you wait him out, he'll have you at no balls and two strikes. If you attack, you might make an out on the first pitch. More teams now are trying to attack him early. And when he's sharp and when he's on, which is most of the time, you're going to have a quick ballgame.

A few other pitchers can do that, if they have the control. There are so many pitchers who have gotten their asses chewed out if they give up an 0-2 hit. I've been with managers who said if you give up a 0-2 pitch, I'm fining you. Some of the pitchers rebelled. At 0-2, they'd throw it up against the screen and glare over: There, he ain't getting a hit now.

There is a lot of hollering that goes on when a pitcher gives up an 0-2 hit. I'm kind of guilty of it myself at times. But not when Maddux is pitching. He knows more than I do.

DOGFIGHT IN SAN DIEGO

We won the pennant in '98 by 18 games. We swept the Cubs in the division series and gave up just four runs. For the NLCS, we had the big series with San Diego. That was one of the loudest parks we'd been to. They had Ken Caminiti, Tony Gwynn, Wally Joyner, Steve Finley and Greg Vaughn. Their pitching staff was Kevin Brown, Sterling Hitchcock and Andy Ashby. Trevor Hoffman was the closer. That was a good team. There are no bad teams once you reach the postseason.

In Game 1 at Turner Field, there was a two-hour rain delay. Caminiti hit a solo shot off Ligtenberg in the 10th for a 3-2 win. I've always felt long rain delays affect the home team a lot more than the visiting team. You're at home and so you tend to want to *be* at home. If you're the visiting team, all you have to do is go back to the hotel. That's no big deal.

We went down 0-3. We won Games 4 and 5 in San Diego. We brought in Greg Maddux in Game 5 to relieve in the last inning, and he got a save. I'll never forget it. We brought him in, and the place in San Diego was going nuts. Maddux always throws 86 or 87 mph; I look up on the board, and he's throwing 91 mph, because he knows he only has to pitch one inning. He comes in and says, "Hey, man, this is cool."

"Really?" I said.

"Yeah, you can just let it fly," he said. "You don't have to set up anybody for later." If you wanted Maddux to close, I guarantee he'd save 40 or 50 games. The possibility that he might relieve that night was discussed before the game. Once again, we were in that sense of urgency. We were down three games to one. There was no tomorrow when he saved that game. Actually, they brought in Kevin Brown in relief in that game, too, and Michael Tucker hit a three-run home run off him.

We played well in San Diego. We played a good series. It was hard fought, with an excitement and energy. A lot of those games went back and forth. The scores were up a little more. But once again, if you look at the numbers of our starting pitchers, they were good. San Diego went on to play the Yankees and got beat. Trevor Hoffman was a great reliever and one of the best I ever saw. When he came in, you pretty much got the sense that the ballgame was over. That club had a lot of personality and a lot of fight. But so did we.

In Game 2, they made a big deal out of the fact that there were a lot of empty seats at Turner Field. Only 43,000 showed up for a National League Championship Series game. I guess we're spoiled. We're all getting spoiled, but I'd much rather be spoiled that way.

We were in World Series in '95 and '96. We made the NLCS in '97 and '98. There might be an error or a badly located pitch or a strikeout when it's not needed. That's not an excuse, that's just the way it is. And there shouldn't be any excuses made, because we were damned good. It may not be until it's over that people will realize what's been accomplished here. But this will go down in history as one of the great runs, from any sport.

SEVENTH INNING:
THE TIMES THAT TRY

Just before spring training in 1999, we were hit with the terrible news that Andres Galarraga was out for the year to treat cancer they found in a bone in his lower back. When something like that happens, it tends to put everything into perspective. We all went over on the team bus to visit him at his home in West Palm Beach. The Big Cat was still moving around pretty good, and he was in great spirits. It's hard to imagine a big, strong son of a gun like that going down. That was an emotional time for everybody. It kind of lets you know that a hanging breaking ball isn't necessarily all that important.

Then Ligtenberg went down with a tear in his right elbow, and he was lost for the year. That one came as a complete surprise. Light was pitching and he felt some kind of pain in his elbow. I figured he was just going through some spring training things, that it wasn't anything drastic. Then the next day we found out he was going to need a new ligament in his elbow. It was shocking because there wasn't anything leading up to it that indicated there was something going on. When we lost Light that left a pretty big hole in our bullpen because he was a proven closer.

Ligtenberg, in this whole scenario, has gone kind of unnoticed. He just quietly did his job—breaking out with 30-something saves and being an effective reliever whether he closed or set up. Whatever role you put Kerry in, he responded. You could not tell the difference in his pitching or his mound presence; everything stayed the same. He was the type of guy who didn't say a lot, just went about his business. Very professional, first-class guy.

John Rocker had already put in his bid to become our closer before Ligtenberg was injured in spring training. Rocker had established himself as the setup guy in '98. In spring training, he came up and told me, "I want to close." I told him to relax, that Ligtenberg was our closer. "I'm going to be your closer," he said. "I'm going to close." Then Light blew his elbow out, and Rocker *did* step in to close.

He didn't have the antics then, but that sure as hell changed as the year went on. It became a whole show in itself. We're talking about more security in New York than the President of the United States. It was unbelievable. I'll tell you what, he could draw a crowd. But he was one of the more coachable guys around. We studied film together and studied mechanics. He pitched with his thumb busted up and bleeding. He would always split open this callous on his pitching thumb, and it wouldn't heal. Yet he continued to go out and pitch and save games.

That bullpen was a bit unusual. We had Kevin McGlinchy, a rookie who made the club out of spring training and had a real good first half. I think what happened in his case is that you always have to be careful about young pitchers who get caught up in the big-league environment. They get carried away with it to the point that their work ethic starts to decline. And then he got hurt. I can see how McGlinchy got hurt, because he never worked at avoiding it. Some people mature at different points in time. Some people need a drastic wake-up call as opposed to a little one. That was really the only time he pitched well, the first half of that season. And you haven't heard from him since, really. Maybe he'll resurface, but you don't know.

We traded Denny Neagle to Cincinnati in the off season and picked up Mike Remlinger, who became the top setup guy in the National League. When Rem came here, we basically simplified his game. He had an excellent fastball. He had a so-so breaking ball that was inconsistent. The way he basically pitched was hard and harder and hardest: hard fastball and hard breaking ball. There were two things we concentrated on: a fastball down and away, and a change-up. He threw his fastball anywhere from 91 to 93 mph; he threw his change at 85 mph, which is the speed of a lot of pitchers' fastballs. He developed the change into an outstanding pitch. And that basically turned him into a fastball, change-up pitcher with an occasional breaking ball.

That change-up became a huge weapon for him, and he threw it in the biggest clutch situations you could think of. I remember a playoff game in Houston where the bases were loaded with a 3-1 count on the hitter. He dropped a change-up for a swing-and-miss and then got him out on the fastball.

Mike was 10-1 that year, 2.37 ERA, and he pitched in 73 games, which was almost every other game. He was very durable. Bobby and I always had to watch using him too much because he was so effective, so automatic, that you had to fight the tendency to keep on bringing him in. You knew when he came into a game that he was going to get you to the closer. We always gave Mike the option of a day off, just like we do all our relievers.

We also got Terry Mulholland that year. We'd admired him from across the field for quite some time. Terry was one of the real good pitchers with the Phillies when they were strong in the early '90s. I was with him at the All-Star Game in Baltimore, and he was a class act. He was a pitcher who had an upbeat tempo, always on the attack.

You could not steal on him. If you got off first base just a hair, he could pick you off. He had a step-off move that was as good as anything I've ever seen. I told him to teach it to all our left-handed pitchers and then teased him that I'd take credit for it. He tried. He could show them how to do it, but they couldn't do it with the quickness he had. That's just something you can't teach. That's something he developed on his own.

GOING DOWN UNDER

Smoltzie's elbow bothered him all year. Even though it hurt him to throw, he only missed five or six starts. In early August, he was down in the bullpen trying to loosen up his elbow. He started throwing, and he started throwing low three-quarter to side-arm. He turned around and said, "See there, Leo?"

"What, John?"

"My elbow doesn't hurt when I throw from there," he said.

I nodded at him. "Well, okay, why don't you try a few more?" He threw some more, and said his elbow still didn't hurt. So I said, "Why don't you try it in a game?"

He turned around and looked at me. "Well, do you think it will work?"

"Absolutely," I said. "You've got live action on your pitches. Your slider's good. Everything's the same except it's coming from a different angle. The only thing that won't work is your change-up. But you can go to a sinker from there."

I went to Bobby. "Hey, Smoltzie's going to be dropping down in his next start."

"Really?" he said.

"Yeah," I told him. "His elbow doesn't hurt from there. It only hurts from up top."

He said, "Well, Leo, what do his pitches look like?"

"They're *nasty*."

"Well, do it," he said.

The next day Smoltzie came down to the bullpen and did it again, throwing low three-quarter. He had two practice sessions and took a day off. Then he started against Houston. He dropped to low three-quarter and shut them down. I'll never forget Craig Biggio saying, "We'd heard he was gonna drop down, but I didn't expect anything as nasty as this."

As a pitching coach, you can't be afraid to say, "Let's give it a shot. If your elbow doesn't hurt from there and your pitches look good from there, let's go ahead and do it." The thing that really puts John in a special category is, number one, that he went ahead and did it. Number two, he trusted that he could make it work in the middle of a pennant race against a team as good as Houston.

Smoltzie stayed down there the rest of the year and pitched effectively. He made 29 starts and finished 11-8. He would have never made those 29 starts pitching overhand. John even broke out some knuckleballs that year. You know how a hitter gets his first hit and gets to keep the ball? Well, when he got his first strikeout on the knuckleball, I had the umpire throw it into our dugout and we kept it for him.

You can use all the adjectives you want in describing what Smoltzie did that year. And it wasn't like he was experimenting with a second-division team. We were neck and neck with the Mets in a pennant race. He was not afraid to do it between the white lines under pressure situations.

That's just John Smoltz. Greatest arm, greatest pure stuff I've ever coached. Greatest pitcher, Maddux. Greatest arm, Smoltz. Most tough-minded individual and most consistent in all phases of the game, Glavine. Greatest young pitcher, Avery.

ROCKIN' IN NEW YORK

We were locked in a tight race with the Mets all year and had a little added drama there courtesy of John Rocker. Sometimes you wanted to tell John to shut up. Then, many times, you'd say, "That's the way to go!" Let's face it, he was the closer and we needed him to win games. And let me tell you something, he was at his best in New York.

Rocker threw hard. He had a big breaking ball and a smaller one. He'd use the smaller one when he got behind in the count and use the bigger one when he got ahead. It's a little misleading that all he threw was gas. He threw hard, but he had good breaking stuff, too. Rock was very coachable. We'd look at film together, look at mechanics. He'd work on his pitches. Sometimes he'd be working on his pitches, and suddenly he'd go ballistic. I'd just walk out of the bullpen and tell him, "I'm not listening to this crap. If you can't control yourself better than this, then the hell with it." There was a lot of upside to John Rocker. But putting up with what comes with it starts to wear on you. Rocker's a very intelligent guy. There was some days when you loved him, and some days when you wanted to kill him.

He called me "Boss Man." I called him "Johnny Rocket." I had many different approaches in coaching Rocker. One was being firm and telling him right out to shut up. Believe me, we had some very animated conversations. Not only when we were practicing, but on the mound.

When we played Houston in the division series, he came in the 10th inning with the bases loaded, nobody out. I was thinking, man, we're never going to get out of this. I went to the mound to talk to him. The Astrodome was going nuts.

He was out there screaming in his glove, which he used to do all the time. And when I got to the mound, I said, "First thing you've got to do is shut up." He pulled the glove down and looked at me, made eye contact. And then I told him he was the best relief pitcher in the National League, the only one who could get out of this with no runs because he could strike out the side. I told him that it starts with the first pitch and the first hitter; once you get the first pitch, then you get the second. I used psychology on him, I blew smoke. And, by God, he struck out the first batter. Then the next hitter was a great play by Walt Weiss at short that got the force at home. The third guy popped up. Inning over.

Rocker would come flying in from the bullpen, running like crazy. The music would start blasting, "I want to rock!" I'll tell you what, it was something to see. Terry Mulholland was a funny guy. He was sitting next to me one time when Rocker came in. Terry said, "Well, Leo, here we go." The crowd's standing up and Rocker's throwing 100 mph warming up, and grunting and groaning and hollering. Terry said, "Leo, there ain't a darned thing you can do about it now. It's out of your hands. Sit back and enjoy the ride. Wherever it may take us."

PUSHED TO THE WALL

Rocker's performance in Game 3 saved that Houston series for us. But he wasn't the only story from that game. We'd lost Game 1; then Millwood threw a one-hitter to win Game 2 5-1, one of the greatest games ever pitched for us in the playoffs. As I've said, there's a sense of urgency in a best-of-five. That tied the series at one to one. After Rocker pitched those two innings in Game 3, we got the lead in the top of the 12th, and Millwood came in to close it out for us.

We used Maddux in relief that game, too. There you are again, a best-of-five. Is there any better example of why they're so crazy? You're in the 12th inning and you've had two starters pitch in relief? Millwood went one inning. And had just as good stuff in that one inning as he did in his shutout the day before. His stuff was phenomenal. And he did it with a lot of fastballs. He stuffed them. It was very efficient and very powerful.

The Mets were next. And Rocker? He dominated their lineup. Six games, 0.00 ERA, two saves, nine strikeouts. When he was in there, they had no chance. He had them swinging over breaking balls, swinging and missing fastballs. His control was good. Once again, he always rose to the occasion against any team that had "New York" on their jersey. Which is odd. New York is my favorite city to go to. I love New York.

In Game 2, Rocker pitched the eighth and then Smoltz came in to close. He struck out Bobby Bonilla to end the game. Some people were already talking about converting Smoltzie into a closer, but there was no plan to do that down the road. The only reason that happened was because he injured his elbow.

You're talking about special people here. Maddux, Kevin Millwood, Glavine. And then Smoltzie. Those guys would do anything to win. When Maddux first got here, he said, "Don't ever be afraid to use me in a four-man rotation. It doesn't bother me a bit."

And Smoltzie told me not to be afraid to use him to relieve in the postseason. And Millwood said, "Shoot, yeah, I can go." He would look at you and go, "I'm ready, dude." You know, Mr. John Wayne. Those are special people with enormous talent and special make-up.

Glavine beat the Mets in Game 3, 1-0. He was in trouble two different times; he'd bend, but not break. What's characteristic of Tom Glavine is this: with two runners on base and less than two outs, he has the best record in baseball for not allowing them to score. That's Tommy—bend but don't break, and don't give in to the strike zone.

I saw Tommy Glavine walk a batter with the bases loaded one time to get to the next hitter. It was Kevin Mitchell, when he was with Cincinnati. Tommy was down 1-0 with the bases loaded and two out in the first inning. He threw a change-up on a 3-2 pitch, low and outside, and Mitchell didn't swing. He walked him. They scored. And everyone was going, oh, geez! I knew what he was doing. He walked Kevin Mitchell on purpose. He got the next guy out and retired the next 18 in a row and won 5-2. Now, any other pitcher would have given in and thrown a strike. And if Mitchell had gotten a hit, you'd be blown out in the first inning. I always told Glavine, "Look, if the bases are loaded, you still have a base open."

"Well, where in the hell is that?" he said.

"Home plate." That's a way of saying don't give in just because the bases are loaded. I saw Glavine walk a hitter in spring training, then pitch around a hitter to get to the next guy. He was practicing.

Tommy Glavine threw a couple of 1-0 games in the postseason, once in Houston and another in Enron a couple of years later. He threw mostly fastballs and change-ups. In the game at Enron Field, he threw 80-something pitches and not a single breaking ball.

And Tommy revolutionized the game, too, when he started to throw inside change-ups in addition to outside change-ups. Guys had never thrown inside change-ups to hitters before. He throws it to a right-handed hitter and they swing right through it. That didn't come into play, though, until 2001. In '99, he didn't do that. Tommy is tough and tough-minded. The Iceman. A real professional. And a Hall of Famer.

The 1-0 win against the Mets in '99 was in Shea Stadium. Glavine always told me, and it's ironic now, that he loved pitching in Shea Stadium. He always pitched successfully there. Tommy very rarely had a bad game at Shea, and that might have played a part in his decision to sign with the Mets.

Game 5 went 15 innings. It was raining like hell in New York, and McGlinchy ended up losing the game. Ventura hit a grand slam home run and stopped at first, so only one run counted and we lost 4-3.

We brought him in because we had used all our pitchers. We could have used one of our starters, but we had the lead in that series and so there was no sense of urgency. For example, when we used our starters in Houston, that series was tied 1-1. And it was a best-of-five. Against the Mets, we were just hoping McGlinchy could get us through an inning or two. The mound was mess. It was raining like heck. We're trying to clinch it. We end up losing the game, but we didn't feel that bad about it, knowing we still had a three-to-two lead in the series and had Millwood coming up. We weren't going to burn out our starting rotation to win that game.

We won Game 6 10-9. What a crazy game. We had a big lead, 5-0 in the fifth inning. We had it perfectly set up. They scored three in the sixth off Millwood, but we scored two in the bottom half of the inning. We brought in John Smoltz to relieve in the seventh. We thought that was it. But they banged Smoltzie around. Bobby and I looked at each other when the Mets tied it up and said, "How in the hell did that happen?"

It happened quick, maybe in five minutes; it wasn't like John was getting deep into the count. You have so much confidence when Smoltz is on the mound that you don't ever think he's going to give up a run. And before you know it, we're in a mess. And then you have Andruw Jones taking a ball four to win the game with the bases loaded in the 11th inning. And we're off to another World Series.

SWEPT

Look at our starting pitching in the World Series against the Yankees in '99. We lost 4-1 in the first game. In the eighth inning, we were up 1-0 with Maddux pitching. There was a bunt situation. Brian Hunter was playing first base and he couldn't get the ball out of his glove. We had to have an out there. It would have given us the opportunity to walk Jeter. But we didn't get the out, and the bases were loaded with nobody out. We had Jeter and Paul O'Neil and Bernie Williams coming up. With the bases loaded and nobody out and Maddux pitching, you're trying to get a double play with the sinker. It didn't happen.

In Game 2, Millwood had a difficult game and we lost 7-2. In Game 3, Tommy's ahead 4-2 in the eighth inning. It's two out, a man on and Chuck Knoblauch at the plate. Knoblauch hits a fly ball to right field. I stand up and go, "All right!" I thought it was an out. The ball just went over the fielder's glove, right over the "314" sign. Tied the game at four.

The second-guessers asked, why did you leave him in? Why didn't you take him out? Well, Tommy had them eating out of his hands. He wasn't tired. His pitch count wasn't high. If we'd brought in a reliever and Knoblauch had knocked it out, they would've asked, why did you pull Glavine, he was pitching so well?

We're down 3-0 in the series when Smoltz takes the mound for Game 4 at Yankee Stadium. Smoltzie is warming up in the bullpen, and he's not throwing side-arm. He's coming in over the top. Now, he hasn't been pitching from over the top for two or three months. I looked over and said, "Smoltzie, what are you doing?"

He said, "I'm over the top today, Leo. I've gotta win, *we've* gotta win."

He goes into that game with a 90-something mph fastball, a nasty slider and a nasty split-finger. See, below three-quarter, he couldn't throw a split. But he needed the split against the good left-handed hitters the Yankees had. He goes into the seventh inning and he's down 3-1, only because of a couple of defensive lapses. And he's got 11 strikeouts. Somebody told me it was the most strikeouts in seven innings ever in a World Series game. Smoltzie comes out of that game down 3-1. He says, "Don't take me out, don't take me out."

I said, "John, we're going to have to try to get some runs. We've only got two innings left."

I didn't think the Yankees had the best team in '96. But they had best team in '99. Even so, we pitched three of those games more than well enough to win them.

UNDER THE KNIFE

Just before spring training in 2000, Smoltzie underwent Tommy John surgery on his right elbow. When we broke camp, it was the first time we'd left spring training without one of our horses coming out of the gate with us. It was a little strange. John Smoltz is the one I've been around the longest, counting the minor leagues and the big leagues.

All the others have always teased me: Mad Dog, Glav, Millwood, Avery. Glavine would look at me and go, "Well, Smoltzie's always been your favorite."

"No," I'd say. "I like you all equally."

Mercker was the same way: "Why don't you holler at Smoltzie the way you holler at me? You don't because he's your favorite."

You know what? Merck was right. Smoltzie *has* always been my favorite.

John made it his goal to come back by the postseason, which is unheard of for that kind of surgery. He started throwing off the mound, and he was throwing extremely well. He wanted to get ready by the first of September to be eligible for the postseason roster. But we all knew that wasn't going to happen. You'd watch him throw—which was a part of his rehab process with his elbow—and you'd go, yeah, I think he could.

I'll tell you what, though, you can practice all you want. But that ain't being in a game. The injury hadn't had enough time to completely heal. Smarter heads prevailed. Common sense. And because it's his career.

You know what, though? He told me later he always knew in the back of his mind that he wasn't going to make the postseason roster. But that was his motivational tool for the rehab, for his work ethic. It gave him something to shoot for. That's the way John is. I've seen him get bored in a regular-season game. His biggest games always occurred at the end of a losing streak or when the game meant even more than it normally did. That was his motivation for his rehab. It gave him something to fight for.

TAKE THE NO. 7 TRAIN

In 2000, we won 95 games and finished one game up on the Mets. The pitching staff led the majors in ERA for the fourth straight season. Tommy led the majors with 21 wins, and Mad Dog was 19-9; he got a total of 15 runs in his nine losses that year.

We picked up John Burkett in spring training; he was awesome and finished 10-6. We saw Burkett in Venezuela. We went down there for spring training because they were honoring Galarraga. Burkie pitched two innings against us, went three up and three down, three up and three down. We got wind that he was being let go by Texas. Bobby liked what he saw and I liked what we saw.

Burkie was always one of the better pitchers we faced in the '90s. Pitchers, when they start getting banged around later in their career after they've had success, they'll start pitching away from their fastball and try to trick guys. They end up going to a bunch of junk. All we did was put more emphasis on the fastball, put more emphasis on the straight change. Now, velocity means absolutely nothing on a fastball. Location does.

MADDUX, MAZZONE AND GLAVINE AT THE 2000 ALL-STAR GAME.

And Burkie was sneaky quick. The gun might not register high, but it's a lot quicker.

He had a big slow curve that was an outstanding pitch for him; he made hitters look sick with it. It all got back to throwing more fastballs. He began to throw as many fastballs as Maddux does, and that's a lot. It's a little bit of an illusion, but Maddux throws more fastballs than any other pitcher we've ever had. They move, but it's all fastballs.

So Burkie started throwing a lot of fastballs on the out-side corner. And he started banging it consistently. Then came

the other stuff behind it. And before you know it, he had simplified his game and narrowed his pitches down to three:
fastball, breaking ball, change. The slider he threw was getting
hit on a consistent basis, so we damned near eliminated it. He
became extremely effective. I remember one time he pitched a
game in Pittsburgh. Their hitters were frustrated. One of them
told me, "Where the hell's all this junk he's supposed to be
throwing?" That kind of made us all feel pretty good.

Burkie was very professional. A class act. Tremendous in
the clubhouse. One of the funniest guys you'd ever want to be
around.

Millwood was injured that year also. His shoulder was
bothering him all year and Kevin wasn't a hundred percent.
There wasn't anything major wrong, but it was enough to affect his pitching. Kevin Millwood, even in that year with a
record of 10-13, always gave his team a chance to win. That's
all you can ask of your starting pitcher, that he gives you the
chance to win the ballgame. And Kevin, whether he was a
hundred percent or a little less than a hundred percent, always
gave his team a chance to win.

This was the year of Rocker and the *Sports Illustrated*
article that set off all the controversy. Rock started the year on
a two-week suspension imposed by the commissioner for his
comments to *Sports Illustrated*. I read it and just went, oh, my
gosh. If that was a way to try to bring attention to yourself,
that was not a good way to do it. Whatever reasons, however it
was interpreted, there was tremendous reaction all over the
country and especially in New York. I'll give him credit for
one thing—it made him pitch better. It was all part of the
package and the motivation. The more controversy he stirred

up, the better he pitched. That's an unusual motivational tool.

After he made all his comments about New York and the No. 7 train, there was a tremendous amount of security when we went to Shea Stadium. The fans couldn't wait for him to come in, especially if it was a save situation, which it normally was. We'd be sitting in the dugout and he'd come flying out of the bullpen in New York. Then the beer bottles and the batteries and everything else would come raining down.

When they renovated the visitors' bullpen in Shea, they put a canopy over it to keep pitchers from getting hit from stuff tossed down from the upper deck. So Rocker did help with the renovations of the bullpen in Shea.

There were cops everywhere, dogs coming through the clubhouse checking lockers and everything. It went on and on. And when he came into the game, it was lights out. John Olerud was one of the best hitters we faced over the years; Rocker would pitch against Olerud and Robin Ventura, and they had no chance.

He'd come in after striking out the side and holler up at the crowd, "I've just struck out your three best hitters!" He's screaming to the people, making a face at them, and you'd have to pull him down into the dugout and tell him to shut up.

I can't figure out what that was about. In a lot of ways, you liked him and you could enjoy discussions with him and working with him. But there were a lot of times you went, what's going on here? You just tried to react and coach accordingly. I'm sure a lot of guys in the clubhouse wouldn't try to talk to him or whatever. It's tough to explain, really. Like I said, it wasn't difficult to work with him. Intelligent kid. When it came to watching film, talking about mechanics and getting guys out, he was great. Then he'd explode sometimes and I'd just leave, I'd walk off. Then at times we'd have some very unusual conversation going back and forth, and then normal conversations about pitching.

It got to be a distraction in the clubhouse. The professionalism in the clubhouse, and the professionalism of the manager and the organization, downplayed it to a point where you tried to protect everybody. Basically, I thought we did one hell of a good job with that.

DEAD IN THE WATER

The division series in 2000 against St. Louis is the most disappointed I've felt during this entire 12-year run. It left me with the emptiest feeling because of the way everything happened. We didn't play well. The whole thing was set up in the first game with Maddux pitching in the first inning in St. Louis. A ball in left center was not caught that should have been. And it snowballed from there. That gave the Cardinals the confidence they needed. They went, "Wow! We've just got six runs off Maddux in the first! If we can do that to him, we can do that to anybody."

And that whole thing started in the first inning of the first game. Basically, we were never in it. Even in the third game at home, the first pitch Millwood threw was a home run to Fernando Vina.

If you had to look to a low point during this entire run in Atlanta, that series was it. It was a more empty feeling than when you lost the World Series. It felt like you'd just wasted 95 wins. And you walked away with a bad taste in your mouth. You just didn't like what happened.

There have been so many highs, but that was what you would call dead in the water.

A Trip to the Mound ...

The role of the catcher is critical. What we want out of the catcher is a good setup, a good presentation to his pitcher of the strike zone and a good presentation to the umpire of the strike zone. If we can take care of those three things, there will be fewer runners who can get to first base for a catcher to have to throw out.

When the catcher puts the sign down, he's making a suggestion. Not the decision. I don't want the pitcher coming in and saying he didn't want to throw that pitch. It just eliminates all excuses. We want the pitcher taking full responsibility for what goes on.

To give an example, Smoltzie was pitching against the Orioles in interleague play one time. The Orioles had runners on second and third with two out. Andruw Jones was in center field; there was a line shot hit to center and Andruw somehow missed it. Smoltzie felt he hadn't run hard after the ball after he misjudged it. Two runs scored and it put Baltimore ahead 2-1.

Smoltzie came into the dugout and said, "Look, we've all got to bust our butt; I know I'm out there busting *my* butt!"

I called Smoltzie over and had him sit down next to me. "Just be quiet for a second, okay?" I said. "Look, you're upset, right?"

"Yeah, I'm out there busting my butt."

"Let me put it to you like this," I said. "Let's think about this. There were runners on second and third. There were two outs. There were no balls and two strikes on the hitter. The hitter was the opposing pitcher. And he made solid contact. Now whose fault is it that those two runs scored?"

See, you always remind them to take full responsibility for what happens out there on the field. And you bring those examples up to them, not in a mean way or derogatory way but in a discussion in the dugout. Of course, you've got to use a little tact.

I tell the catchers that they have to be the pitcher's best friend. Because when that pitcher's out there and he's getting his ass beat around and giving up some runs, he doesn't have any friends out there. He doesn't have any friends in the stands; he doesn't have any friends on the field. The catcher's got to be his best friend and help him get through it.

Javy Lopez and Maddux, that's a whole different story. People have always wondered: why does Javy never catch Greg Maddux? The interesting thing is that Maddux tells the catcher what's coming a lot of times. *He* gives the sign. And Javy can't always pick up the signs. So Maddux is worried that if he throws a pitch with a man on third and crosses up the catcher, the run scores because the catcher didn't know what was coming. And that's it. Plus the fact that if Javy goes zero for two or zero for three, is he still thinking about catching?

See, Javy's a great physical catcher. He's caught Cy Young Award winners and 20-game winners, Glavine and Smoltz. It's just that Maddux is so intricate in his thought processes that he doesn't want any distractions. He can't make the pitch if he's unsure whether the catcher knows that a change-up is coming.

There are little things Maddux does on the mound to give the signs. A few of the other pitchers call some of their pitches. But Maddux has a set of intricate signs, whereas other pitchers will move their heads. Curt Schilling will call a lot of the locations when the hitters aren't looking. The hitter steps out of the box and you can see him making gestures with his face, telling the catcher where he's going. But Maddux goes beyond that.

We always want the catcher's crotch lined up at the corner. Because if his crotch is lined up on the corner, that means half is body is in the strike zone and half is out. You try to eliminate any movement of the catcher's glove. You can be in the middle of the plate, and if you move the glove to the right or the left, a lot of times the umpire will call a ball. You can be right on the corner, just off a hair, and it's called a strike if he doesn't move the glove. We have a saying in our practice sessions: if you hit the catcher's crotch every time, you'll never give up a hit. It sounds kind of crude but if you visualize that, it works. When you're pitching, you have to have a target to lock in on.

To some pitchers, their relationship with the catcher means a lot. To others, they could give a hoot. It all depends on the individuals. John Smoltz could not pitch to Mike Heath. He just couldn't do it. John didn't like the way he tried to handle him. Didn't like it and said so. John loved Greg Olson. Glavine and Smoltzie love Javy. Mad Dog loved Eddie Perez. And Charlie O'Brien was a great catcher. Damon Berryhill was a great catcher, and Greg Olsen was a great catcher.

We've been very fortunate. Sure, some of them were more cerebral than others. But all of them were great physical catchers. Javy's the big power catcher. Eddie Perez was a good defensive catcher, got hurt a lot. Berryhill had a little bit of everything, a little bit of thinking and a little bit of hitting. Greg Olsen had a little bit of everything too. The best defense, of course, was Charlie. The best offense, Javy.

I remember Charlie came into the dugout one time not long after he arrived in Atlanta, and he's shaking his head. And I say, "What's the matter, Charlie?"

"These dudes keep shaking me off," he says.

"Well, we have a saying here, Charlie," I say. "When you put your finger down, you're making a suggestion, not a decision."

He took his mask off and stared at me. It was the dirtiest look I ever got from a catcher. He shook his head and walked down to the other corner of the dugout. I said, "Charlie, you know, the track record ain't too bad around here."

Charlie O'Brien is the greatest catcher I ever saw in terms of picking up pitches. Mad Dog tried to cross him up a couple of times and couldn't do it. Charlie told Maddux, "Tell me where to set up; I won't even call the pitches. Just throw whatever the hell you want to. You ain't gonna mess me up, dude."

Mad Dog kept saying, "I can't get him. I can't make him miss one." That's how good Charlie was. A lot of times, Maddux threw pitches to Charlie O'Brien with men on second and no signs. Charlie caught it, piece of cake. He paid attention. Charlie was a tremendous defensive catcher. And got some clutch hits for us, too.

EIGHTH INNING:
A NEW KIND OF ENDING

The Atlanta Braves have the reputation of a quiet clubhouse. No fights. No mouthing off. Very professional. People who won't fit in don't usually stay very long. Like a sportswriter told me one time, it's a boring team to cover because there's nothing going on; all we do is go out and win. And win with class and professionalism.

By 2001, we were into our third season of John Rocker. You deal with it. But it got to the point that it was such a distraction that something had to be done.

Rocker pitched well that year. He had 19 saves and a 3.09 ERA in 30 games. The controversy and the distractions didn't bother him. But we had the chance to pick up Steve Karsay, whom we'd loved for a long time, and Steve Reed, who was extremely effective at getting out right-handed hitters. And Smoltzie came back from his Tommy John surgery and was coming into the equation in the bullpen.

That was a trade based on acquiring quality depth for our bullpen. John Schuerholz was not going to trade Rocker just to trade him. He got quality in return. That was a good trade whether there was controversy or no controversy.

At the time of the trade, I think Rocker was second in the National League in saves. I don't think he's saved very many since. Once again, Rocker is high maintenance, physically and mentally. What's the difference between then and now? The way he was handled by Bobby Cox, the way we gave him a day or two off when he needed it. There were times when he had to pitch an inning and a third, and he'd have to have his lower back stretched out in the runway in between innings in order to get him back out there for the ninth inning. Because he was so muscular, he had a tough time rebounding sometimes. He was a max effort guy. To say the least.

He stopped pitching effectively once he got to Cleveland. When he went to Texas, it was even worse. There were times here when I'd go out to the mound, and he would tell me what he felt and we would talk about mechanics and checkpoints. We had checkpoints that we used all the time. One was his upper body. When it was leaning too far toward the first base line, he wasn't as effective because it took away the angle of his pitches. I saw him pitch in a game on ESPN one night, and he was leaning toward the first base line. He had that exaggerated upper body lean toward first.

I think the difference was that in Atlanta he was in a very comfortable situation with the manager he was pitching for, and our relationship was fine. He was allowed input into how often we used him.

Being in Atlanta helped because he grew up in Macon. The whole scenario was perfectly set up for him to enjoy a fine career with the Atlanta Braves. There was the shock of being traded, having to leave that environment. And different managers do things in different ways. That probably all played a part in it. We tried in every way to find out how to help him. I don't know what happened after that.

OFFENSIVE EXPLOSION

In 2001, Tommy Glavine finished third in the league in walks allowed. He had 97 that year, way above his career average. Baseball had changed. Mark McGwire and Sammy Sosa had each hit over 60 home runs in 1999. In 2001, Bonds would hit 73 and Sosa 64.

In spring training, there was a lot of talk about the umpires being ordered to call the "real" strike zone, to call the high strikes and not give pitchers wide strikes. Tommy got off to a rough start. In making his adjustments, he tried to accommodate the new strike zone by bringing the ball more across the middle of the plate. It didn't work and so we finally decided that if we had to walk more people, we just would, because walks were better than doubles or triples or home runs. Once again, it comes back to making a positive out of a negative. We tell pitchers it's better to live on the edge than give in to the fat part of the plate. Let's not talk about how many we're going to walk; let's talk about making good pitches.

Let me tell you something: when that strike zone came into play it was pointed at two people: Maddux and Glavine. Because everybody was complaining about them getting a little more edge off the corners. I've never heard of anything more ridiculous in my life. If Barry Bonds doesn't swing, it's a ball.

Remember Avery against Wade Boggs in the World Series? He couldn't get a called strike on him. Or Tony Gwynn. So we understand that, and we accept that because of their abilities and what they've done. Well, it's the same thing with a pitcher. If you've had success over the long haul and you're constantly hitting your target, you deserve the benefit of the doubt.

There was an enormous amount of controversy going on about the strike zones and the catcher's box. We were in a game in Milwaukee and they made the grounds crew re-chalk the catcher's box after the third inning, claiming catchers have to sit a certain distance behind the batter. If you watch other games, it all varies. It was just an interruption to the game that wasn't necessary. It was just ridiculous.

You very rarely see a high strike called and if you do, it's a breaking ball that didn't break. There are more high breaking balls called than high fastballs. It just doesn't make any sense to me that a pitcher should be rewarded for a mistake. By the same token, if you're down and away on the black or inside on the corner, and you're right there on the edge, you're not rewarded for great control. It gets kind of crazy.

In trying to adapt to the strike zone, you either don't get as many pitches called, or else your adjustment is too much over the middle. When you're talking about adjustments with Glavine and Maddux, you're talking minute adjustments. If you're great, the small things become huge. We're talking inches. We're talking the width of the ball. We're talking about the black of the plate. We're talking about a third of the plate. We're talking about an inch off the plate. It plays a huge factor in their effectiveness.

There's no question that Glavine and Maddux were poster children for this whole thing because of their great control, and everybody claiming that the Braves pitchers go a little more off the edge of the plate than anybody else. I don't think those people would be complaining if those types of pitchers were on their staff.

You can get into too much BS about it. We were in Arizona. Bobby had been thrown out of the game. Remlinger hurt himself and I went out to the mound. Angel Hernandez was umpiring. There'd been a game in Montreal where Tommy pitched and Hernandez umpired, and Tommy started in every once in a while on what he thought were bad calls. And Hernandez hollers out that there aren't going to be any corners. We don't really appreciate an umpire hollering out that there aren't going to be any corners.

It happened again that night in Arizona. He hollered out that there weren't going to be any corners called that night, only north and south. He hollered it again when an opposing hitter was in the box. So I'm out to the mound to check on Rem when Hernandez came out. Our catcher, Henry Blanco, was out there egging it on. He asked Hernandez, where was the 2-0 pitch? Hernandez said it was a little outside. Blanco asked, how about the 1-0? Hernandez said it was a little inside.

So I turned around and said, "They were all strikes. Your right hand is going up, and then you're stopping it and bringing it back down."

He suggested that I should never discuss the strike zone with him. And I said the Atlanta Braves did not like him yelling out at our pitchers that he wasn't calling corners. "You can call the game that way and you can believe it in your mind, but don't ever shoot your mouth off about it."

I may have said a few other things, too. It's only the second time I've ever been tossed from a game.

I also got thrown out in my first year with the Braves. I went out to talk to Charlie Leibrandt, who said his strike zone was getting squeezed. Jerry Crawford was the umpire. He said, "Hey, what's going on out here?"

I said, "Well, your strike zone looks a little tight."

He said, "Get the hell out of here. Who the hell are you?"

And he was right. I was nobody, you know? It was one of the dumbest things I've ever done. So when I came into the dugout, Bobby said, "Don't ever do that again. You might have been able to do that with umpires in minor leagues, but you're not going to intimidate anybody here."

THE EXPLOSION OF OFFENSE

We led the league in 2001 with a 4.08 staff ERA, the first time our staff ERA was over four since the '90 season. It was the offensive explosion in major-league baseball. Who would have predicted somebody could hit 73 home runs in a season? I think it came from the smaller ballparks. I also think that bats are harder, balls are harder. Strike zones got a little smaller.

Maddux told me that when he was playing for Chicago early in his career, Andre Dawson would hit home runs to the opposite field during batting practice. It was so unusual that everybody would stop and look. Now it's a regularity. I re-member one time *Maddux* hit an opposite-field home run off

Kevin Brown. He came into the dugout and said, "I can't do that. What am I doing? I can't *do* that."

I used to be able to put a dent in a baseball with my thumb, or at least push on the seam, or push on the cover and get a little indentation or something. If I did that now, I'd break my thumb. Its just the technology getting better, and the guys being bigger and stronger.

What I don't understand is all the Tommy John surgeries that are happening now to pitchers who hardly pitch at all. You start seeing pitchers, young pitchers, who had the surgery. Ligtenberg had it, and he didn't pitch many innings. Odalis Perez had it, and he hadn't acquired a lot of innings. I remember a couple of kids in spring training who were sent down and they wound up having it, and they hadn't accumulated any innings.

I think there's a case to be made that they're overloading their ligaments and their tendons when they bulk up to get big and strong. But I'm not an expert on it. I don't think it helps a pitcher to bulk up. I'm from the old school. There used to be a saying: loose and live. I think the injuries occur from being tight and restricting yourself. Rocker was high maintenance physically because he was such a built-up guy as far as hitting the weights.

Personally, I'd like to see the pitching mound raised. It would lower the risk of arm injury. Any time that you have more momentum going down the hill, then I think you lower the risk of arm injury. And since you're investing a lot of money in pitchers, that makes sense.

I know for a fact that pitchers love throwing on a higher mound more than they do a lower one. The slope is steeper.

I'll tell you, a hundred percent of the pitchers will take a steeper slope. They lowered the mound in '68 because of the domination of pitching, because of Bob Gibson and Don Drysdale. Now, I think you have to have an equalizer of some sort on the other side. Things have favored the offense over the last few years.

It's also frustrating when a guy hits a ball, and you say, oh man, he didn't hit it good. And you look up and it's gone. I remember seeing an instant replay on ESPN, a guy broke his bat on a swing and the ball still went over the center field wall. When I see a guy carrying the handle of his bat down the line and the ball's out of the park, you've just got to say, whoa, wait a minute here. Something's not right.

BURKIE'S 219.3

Millwood was just 7-7 in 2001 because his arm was bothering him all year. Kevin got to a point where he was trying to get his stuff right, and he was beating himself up. He was frustrated and he started to labor. There are just some times when you say "I need a break." He went a lot further than most pitchers would. I mean, Kevin's a 220-inning guy.

He came in one day and I said, "Kevin, are you okay?"

"I can't go no more," he said. "Dude, I just need to give it a breather for a while." Kevin would go out there when he wasn't feeling good, so that told us something. He had to take a couple of months off; we shut him down for a while. And then he was able to come back in the following year, 2002. His arm didn't hurt any more, and what did he do? Become one of the best pitchers in the National League.

When spring training started, we penciled Burkett into the starting rotation right out of the get-go. I told him, "You're going to pitch 220 innings this year, and we're going to simplify our game. You're going to throw a lot more fastballs this year." In other words, you're not telling them how to do it, you're working with them on *how* to do it, giving a few tips here and there. Being the professional that Burkie is, he started getting results with a fastball that was 85 miles an hour, a fastball that looked extremely quick. Burkie ended up third in the National League in ERA that year.

We were going up the tunnels at the end of the season, and I said, "Burkie, I have to apologize to you."

He goes, "What for, Leo?"

"I said that you were going to pitch 220 innings this year. You only pitched 219 and a third."

I go into every season thinking that our starting pitchers are all going to pitch 220 innings, with the exception of your fifth starter, who gets skipped over every so often because of the schedule. I really and truly believe that it's going to happen, and then work toward that. The record I'm most proud of is the innings pitched by our starting staff. Not the 20-game winners or the Cy Youngs. The thing is, when you have the innings pitched, everything else is taking care of itself.

Jason Marquis began to spot-start for us. And he had one of the greatest games I've ever seen pitched. It was in Los Angeles, on a spot start, and he did an awesome job, two hits and no runs over six innings. And then one time in Milwaukee, Burkett got sick and couldn't pitch, so Jason moved up a day early and completely dominated Milwaukee.

There was a common denominator in those two starts: he didn't know he was going to pitch until he got to the park.

That's got to tell you something right there. Jason is at a point where he's already shown he can dominate on a major-league level, so now preparation and the mentality come into play, learning how to do it on a regular basis. What was so impressive about those two games is that he didn't let the count dictate his pitch selection. He threw what he wanted in any situation. That was quite impressive, and now we're hoping we'll see more of that as he matures.

AUTOMATIC FOR THE PEOPLE

Making Smoltzie a closer had nothing to do with the genius of our coaching. It was dictated by how his elbow reacted. He came back in 2001 and began the season on the disabled list. He was activated in May and started five games, then went back on the disabled list. When we activated him again in July, we put him in the bullpen.

That way, he was able to pitch an inning or two and feel great. As opposed to starting and pitching into the fifth or sixth inning, and then having his elbow start to bother him. It just evolved naturally because of circumstance. If pitching an inning or two didn't bother him, it wasn't that difficult to figure out. The only thing I ever told John was to make sure to keep your starter's mentality when you're closing. I wanted him to use all his pitches. That way he'd still be a pitcher, not a thrower.

We also had to make sure that we gave him enough time to recover between appearances until his arm was at full strength. At first, we brought him into games in the middle innings, just to let him get some pitches under his belt in non-pressurized situations. Then, gradually, we added some responsibility to the role that he was about to take over. We eased him into it. And when he did take over, it was lights out. Almost automatic. He was 10 out of 11 in save situations at the end of the year.

That gave us the ability to close with John Smoltz and to set him up with Mike Remlinger, Steve Karsay and Rudy Seanez. None of them threw under 90 mph; Karsay would throw 95, Smoltz would throw 95, Rem would throw 93, Rudy would throw anywhere from 91 to 95. I thought those four, at that particular time, were as good as any bullpen we'd ever had.

When you looked at John Smoltz, as opposed to Rocker and Wohlers, you knew his control was going to be real good. No matter what. If he was going to make a mistake, it would be a mistake down the middle.

Plus, Smoltzie is so reliable and so intimidating that it forced our opponents to play six-inning games. Because Karsay and Remlinger were good, too. And Reed inherited a lot of tough situations that went unnoticed—bases loaded with two out, second and third with two out, first and third with two out—and he would get those big right-handed hitters out. And then he would be out of the game, and we'd have Rem and Karsay and Smoltzie start the innings. Reed did a lot of the dirty work. We had quite a good thing going on down there in the pen.

It dramatically changed the dynamic of our games, simply because it put pressure on the other team to score early. We ran into that same thing against John Wetteland and

Mariano Rivera with the Yankees. You know you have to do something before those guys get in there. Once Smoltzie went into the closer's role, other teams had to get to us early. They had to do something before they saw Karsay or Rem or Smoltzie. And that was a huge advantage, especially when your starting staff includes Maddux and Glavine and Millwood and Burkett.

ANOTHER SWEEP

We drew Houston again in the division series. And where were we going? Enron Field. Where every little popup to left field goes out. I think it's a brutal place to play baseball. They have center field going up a hill, with a flagpole in it.

It's a heck of a hitter's park. A left-handed hitter can fight a pitch off and hit a home run to the opposite field; he doesn't even have to hit it hard. I've seen line drives hit the steel in that left field scoreboard and bounce back to the short-stop. It makes the game a little crazy. Not as bad as Coors Field, but, you know, it can be intimidating for a pitcher.

Maddux started Game 1 and he was down 3-2 in the sixth. We came back and won 7-4, and Smoltzie closed it out. Smoltzie threw all fastballs because he had runs to work with. There are going to be closing situations where he throws more breaking balls, and there are going to be closing situations where he doesn't throw any. With a three-run lead in the ninth against Houston, he threw all fastballs. The next game was 1-0, and Smoltzie pitched the ninth inning of that game throwing fastballs, sliders and splits. So he lets the number of runs he

CELEBRATING THE 2001 DIVISION CHAMPIONSHIP, THE TENTH IN A ROW FOR THE BRAVES, WITH SMOLTZ AND GLAVINE.

has to work with dictate what he's going to throw. That's how good he is.

Glavine started Game 2 and threw all fastballs and change-ups. That's when his inside change-up became a big factor. Bobby noticed that Javy was setting up inside on a right-handed hitter, and you're expecting to see a hard fastball or a sinker. Then he'd throw a straight change, and the batter would swing right through it. A lefty's not supposed to throw a change-up to a right-handed hitter. It's like Ali throwing right-hand leads; it's supposed to leave you vulnerable. But when a hitter sees a pitch coming inside, they always think it's coming in hard. And Glav's change-up was so good and so deceptive, he had them swinging right through it. It takes a toughness to go against the grain, and then to be extremely successful. And that's the greatness of a guy like Glavine.

We swept Houston in three games. Burkie pitched the third game and won 6-2. He went six innings. Then we brought in Reed, then Remlinger, then Karsay, and closed with Smoltz. That was the chain of command we had going down in the bullpen. And it was a darn good one.

Schilling and Johnson

We met the Arizona Diamondbacks in the NLCS, and they had two pretty good pitchers of their own. I thought we played great in the first two games. In the first game you had Greg Maddux going against Randy Johnson, two future Hall of Famers. Arizona won 2-0 and it was a tremendous duel.

We took the second game 8-1 behind Glavine. Early in the game, Tommy sat down and said, "I don't know what to throw Mark Grace when I'm behind in the count."

"What has he hit so far when you had him down in the count?"

"He's hit my slider, base hit," Glav said. "He hit my change-up, base hit."

"You're behind in the count, and you're throwing him a slider and a change-up," I said. "And he's hitting them. Mark Grace is no dummy. You can never go wrong with a sinker down and away, lefty to lefty, regardless of the count."

Sure enough, Mark Grace got up later in the game with the bases loaded and two out. Tommy got behind in the count.

He threw a sinker down and away, and Grace hit a ground ball to second to end the inning and get Tommy out of trouble. He came back to the dugout and said, "Hey, don't be afraid to tell me that a little sooner."

We played great baseball in Arizona, and we came home to Turner Field and booted the ball around. We had four infield errors in Game 3, and it just fell apart. We used seven pitchers. You run into those types of games every once in a while where you have to use everybody. And it goes back to my old theory: If a lot of guys are pitching in games, you're not doing well. Like I've said, I hope I always have three guys coming to me all the time complaining about not getting enough work.

Game 4 was another disaster. Four errors again. An 11-4 loss. That's how you're going to get Maddux out of a game. I didn't think there was any major difference in the way he pitched in Arizona and the way he pitched in Atlanta. It's just that you've got to make plays.

Glavine matched up with Randy Johnson in Game 5, the two premier left-handers of the past couple of decades. Glavine and Johnson are such opposites. Randy Johnson now has great control, and he puts the ball where he wants. He even tinkers with an off-speed pitch. Early in his career, Johnson just overpowered you. He and Schilling are complete pitchers. It's not that they just overpower you; they're *pitching*. People would say you've got to lay off of his slider. Well, that's a heckuva lot easier said than done.

I love the marquee matchups. It was a great game. That was typical whenever those two matched up. Johnson and Glavine had gone at it a couple of times in 2-1 ballgames during the season that were outstanding. We lost, another one-run game, and it put us out of the postseason. The margin of error against Randy Johnson or Curt Schilling is extremely small. By the same token, it's small against our staff, too.

I thought we played well against Arizona on the road. We had a very difficult time at home. And that seemed to be a typical pattern that started in '96. We played extremely well in Yankee Stadium. I don't know why. I don't know if I'm reading more into it than I should. I just know we felt real comfortable on the road.

A TRIP TO THE MOUND …

When I was pitching, if I walked a couple of guys, the manager would come out and say, "Get the bleeping ball over the bleeping plate."

I wanted to look at him and go, "Well, no bleeping shit. I ain't throwing these balls off the plate for the hell of it." So I was taught early how *not* to do it.

As the pitching coach of the Atlanta Braves, I get to meet a lot of people and talk to a lot of people. You wind up being able to get a lot of good tips from the great ones: Jim Kaat, Jim Palmer, Whitey Ford, Sandy Koufax, Don Drysdale, Don Sutton. These are guys I want to talk to about pitching. Because they had great success. I had Jim Palmer watch a practice session with Millwood in Baltimore through some spyglasses to see if he saw any flaws in his mechanics. Nobody knew it.

It is cool to talk to those guys because I grew up watching a lot of them. The thing is, I'm not intimidated by somebody like Don Sutton giving one of our pitchers a tip. If Don

Sutton can't give somebody a tip, who the hell can? A lot of people would say "Get the hell away from my pitchers." Not me. You know, I need to pick up pointers, too. Those are the people I seek out, and they love to do it.

If a pitcher goes out and pitches successfully, that's the important thing. If it comes from people like that, who cares? You try to take advantage of all the tools that are available to you.

But don't give somebody a tip if you don't know what the hell you're talking about. You get a lot of that, too. I remember one time Mark Wohlers had saved 10 games in a row. His next game, he looked different out on the mound. He blew that save, and he didn't blow too many at that time. He just looked different, almost like when you're driving a car and there's too much play in the steering wheel.

Emotions are running high after a game, and I always wait till the next day to talk to a pitcher and kind of shoot the bull. I went up to him and said, "Mark, your delivery looked different yesterday. Were you doing anything different?"

He said, "Well, somebody said that I had to show my butt more to the hitter."

"I didn't tell you that," I said. "I haven't talked to you about your mechanics in more than two weeks because you're shooting lights out. Let's just remember one thing. There are only two pitching coaches on a major-league team. Me and the manager. Those are your two pitching coaches. And you have to be real careful about whose advice you take. If I'm not saying there's something wrong with your mechanics, then there isn't."

Somebody planted a seed that wasn't necessary.

I learned a lot from studying the career of Red Auerbach. I read his philosophies and listened to what he had to say about coaching the Boston Celtics. He always said that the key to successful coaching is changing with the athletes and the times, yet still making sure to get your points across. You have to get the things done that you want to get done within the environment that you're in. That's very similar to what Johnny Sain taught me.

Those are the types of people that I try to draw knowledge from. Nobody knows everything. I want to know what they were thinking, what their philosophies were, how they went about it. That's why I talked to Jim Palmer and had him watch a couple pitchers for me.

I was very fortunate early in my career to learn how *not* to do it. I was taught how *not* to do it by certain individuals whom I thought made a shambles of pitching or made a joke of pitching. Or who really didn't give it the thought process, just cloned what everybody else said and relied on the usual clichés.

The one thing I always told myself was that I was never going to be like that.

NINTH INNING:

GLAVINE'S FINALE

Regardless of the win-loss record, Bobby Cox does a great job every year. When you're down in that dugout and you're in the trenches with him, there is nobody better, regardless of the outcome.

I think the 2001 and 2002 seasons were two of Bobby's best jobs of managing. We won 101 games in 2002, the most in the National League. We got hot in the middle of the year and just hauled ass. Every once in a while, I had to check myself to see how we were doing it. Our pitching staff put up some awesome numbers. The staff ERA was 3.13. You know how you have dreams of sugarplums dancing in your head? For a long time, we flirted with our ERA being under three. Can you imagine a pitching staff ending up with an earned run average that low in this day and age?

The real story from 2002 was our bullpen. Chris Hammond was unbelievable; he finished the year with an 0.95

ERA and was just the third relief pitcher to finish with an ERA under one since 1900. He'd been out of the game three years, but we knew he was very tough against us in the past and we knew he had a great change-up. He was another Greg McMichael, a guy who caught our eye in spring training. He pitched a game against the Twins in Fort Myers where he had them completely off balance.

In working with Hammond, we put his emphasis on the fastball because he had the change. We knew that if his fastball became the equal of his change-up, he had the chance to be really good; if it remained secondary to his change-up, he was going to be so-so. He actually picked up velocity on the fastball, three or four mph, by practicing it and throwing it more.

All of a sudden, his change-up wasn't just good; it was great, because he had a weapon to complement it. Remember, changing speeds isn't just about pulling the throttle; you push it also.

And then you had Darren Holmes, who was a breaking-ball pitcher. Holmsey also picked up velocity on his fastball. Everybody knew he had great breaking stuff. Emphasis was put on the fastball to equal the breaking ball. He started throwing more fastballs than breaking balls and had a great year, 55 appearances and a 1.81 ERA.

Light picked up a lot of innings for us. Spooneybarger was a young kid who showed a lot of promise. Kevin Gryboski did a real good job throwing the sinker. He was having a so-so spring, and then in the second part, just came out of nowhere. Kevin did a great job getting some tough outs with inherited runners. Especially in the first three-quarters of the season.

Pitchers have to adjust to get better, and Kevin needs to up-grade another pitch to go another level higher.

There were three guys in the bullpen with ERAs under 2.00: Remlinger, Hammond and Holmes. The ducks were in order. There was a brief spurt where Remlinger and Hammond weren't available. We played three three-game series and lost every one. The reason for that is we didn't have Hammond and Remlinger to go to—our ducks were out of order. Then when they came back, off we went again.

A Year Unparalleled

We had Smoltzie penciled in as our closer for 2002, but he was back and forth about whether he wanted to go back to starting. He wanted to be with his buddies on the starting staff. Plus, he got frustrated in the NLCS against Arizona—he couldn't get into the games because Schilling and Johnson were shutting us down. "I miss the part of matching up with them right out of the gate," he told me. "In the bullpen, you have to wait and wait and wait. And if I don't get in, I get frustrated because I know we're behind."

He had been a free agent after the 2001 season, and he turned down a huge contract with Yankees (with the guarantee to start) to stay with the Braves. And I'm sure glad he did. He did it because of family and loyalty and being comfortable. He was getting plenty of money with either contract. John's a very family-oriented guy. I think he just feels comfortable. After a while, you can only get so much money.

Smoltzie had one bad inning against the Mets early in the season, which kept his ERA above three. Take out that one inning, and he was about as dominant as it gets. He had a 1.44 ERA after June 14 and converted 35 of 36 save opportunities. Personally, I thought before the season that 40 saves was a lock. He went out and saved 55 games, which broke the National League record. Number one, you had to get into position for him to get all those saves. And number two, once he was in the position to get them, he got them.

With his history as a starter, if he can save 40 or 50 games the next three or four years, that will be his shot at the Hall of Fame.

They talk about having a "closer's mentality," but I think that's overrated. You can have all the mentality you want, but if you don't have the pitches, it's not going to do you any good. You've got to have pitches; you've got to have stuff. I think the opposition looks at Smoltzie and goes: oh, no, here comes a 95 mph fastball, a 91 mph split and a 87 mph slider. He's already in their head before he ever gets started. And then with his control and his pitching, it adds to it.

I have seen pitchers with great stuff who were in a comfort zone in the eighth inning and then couldn't handle the ninth inning. They've made closing such a big deal in the game now. But Alejandro Pena always said it the best: "I don't know what the big deal is. I only have to get three outs, and I can do that with my fastball."

Smoltzie not only has the pitches, he has the mentality. He's a closer with a starter's mentality.

THE MENTOR

Everyone knew, of course, that Glav and Mad Dog were both in the final years of their contracts. We never thought about it. You're thinking about winning games and pitching well. You can't control that stuff anyway, so there's no reason to worry about it. You have to focus: we have games to win, we have a pennant to win. We're all still here, so let's go on and get after them. You can't let the contract enter into your thinking because it will drive you crazy. You've got a job to do, and that's to go out and perform.

We had a young left-hander from Australia named Damian Moss who was going to be in the starting staff. A rookie. I went up to Tommy in spring training and said, "Look, we're gonna double-team Damian Moss. What he's going to hear from me and what he's going to hear from you will be the exact same thing. But when he hears it from you, it's going to have a little more impact because of your track record."

Again, that goes back to Johnny Sain. Johnny always told me that if you're trying to get a point across to a pitcher and you have a great example that you can use, that just makes it easier to get through. My thought process went back to that and then to Tommy.

Mossy wanted to learn. He really wanted to listen. And it paid off for him.

He defied logic at times with the bases on balls. Mossy would put you on the edge of your seat. I told him one time, "I wish you didn't have to make so many clutch pitches." By the same token, he showed a lot of character by not giving in, one small example of Glavine's influence. So we were very happy with Mossy and he did a great job. Mossy was able to come in and take over the number four hole and more than hold his own.

There was a game in Minnesota; he was really outstanding. He had a no-hitter going in St. Louis where he was walking the leadoff guy every inning. Everybody asked why we took him out when he had a no-hitter going. It was because he came into the dugout and told us he was exhausted.

Mossy and Glavine are very similar pitchers. Mossy moved over to the third base side of the rubber so that his pitches wouldn't cut back on him to a right-handed hitter. Mossy has a great change-up and an occasionally good curve. His approach to hitters was very similar to Tommy's. The action on their pitches is similar. It only made sense to put them together.

And Mossy liked it. That's the bottom line. He liked it. He frustrated a lot of hitters. And he frustrated them because he didn't let the count dictate what he was going to throw.

BONDING

We met the San Francisco Giants in the division series. Tommy had a tough time of it in Game 1. We lost 8-5, and the reason for that is that he was too strong. People will think you're crazy for saying that, but that's what happened. It was the strongest he'd been at any point in the season. His fastball was up near 90 mph, and I thought he was making a lot of good pitches. He had good life on his fastball. He never really got banged around; he was nicked here and there.

Tommy's stuff was a lot better than the line score that he had. He kept coming in and telling me, "I'm feeling good, I'm feeling strong. I should be getting better results."

Once you get that strong, you can lose your separation of speeds. When Tommy's pitching, he makes a lot of hitters get off balance. And I didn't see the hitters being off balance. When you feel that strong, it's the natural tendency to go with the power and forget about the change of speeds.

Sometimes you might have a tendency to out-fox yourself. Especially when you feel so good physically, it can give you a false sense of security. In change-up situations, you throw more fastballs instead of going ahead and throwing what you normally would throw. That's not second-guessing what Tommy decided. When pitchers feel that good, they have the tendency to lean that way and that's not wrong. It all gets down to one thing: location. It really doesn't matter what he throws if he locates his pitches.

We came back in Game 2 behind Millwood. We put our usual shift on Bonds where we play three people on the right side of the infield, because you look at all the charts and that's where he hits the ball. We hoped that he would look out there and see that whole left side open and take a shot at it. That would be fine with us. Over the years we've taken a lot of hits from him on line shots up the middle. Or shots to the second baseman, who's playing in short right field. It used to be you could get Bonds out down and away. Now you have to make a great pitch to a great location. I told the pitchers going in—if he makes contact let's have a goal to make him hit it on the ground.

He's such a great hitter. Even the ground balls he hits are hard. If he gets a single the opposite way, nobody's going to get upset. He's just a tremendous talent. He was always real good, and now he's great. I think he can recognize a pitch better than any hitter in the game. It's like what they used to say about Ted Williams—it's his eyesight. He can see it a lot earlier than everybody else. I've never seen a guy just spit on some pitches that could have been a borderline strike.

We've always attacked him. We've always pitched to him more than any other club. But he's on such an incredible level now, I don't know how smart that is. How you get him out, I don't know. We kind of knew how early in his career. Now you pitch to him with nobody on, or when he can't beat you. He's really the only hitter we've faced over 12 years where we can truly say "we don't want any part of him." The key to pitching to Barry Bonds is how you pitch to the ones before he comes up, and then after he comes up.

He hit a solo home run off Smoltzie in Game 2. Smoltzie and him have had a thing going on over the years, it's a one-on-one thing. They challenge each other. One time in Candlestick, Smoltzie struck him out three times. Then next time out, Bonds took him deep twice. They have this connection with one another. If Smoltzie strikes him out, Bonds tips his hat to him. When Bonds comes back and hits a home run, Smoltz tips his hat to him. They get after it. Smoltzie is going to take him on if he's not the tying or winning run. Right now, I'd say it's a 50-50 standoff between them.

That's a classic confrontation. There have been a couple of times when Smoltzie would come in and say, "I don't see how he laid off of that split. I threw him a 91 mph split and he just spit on it." Then there were times when Smoltzie blew him away, and that doesn't happen very often.

In Game 3, Maddux pitched a great game in PacBell Stadium, and we won 10-2. He threw a five-hitter and was just on top of his game. He had them really frustrated. That was a tough season for Mad Dog. He hurt his back early on. It was a high hopper to the mound. He went up, made the play, turned to first base and threw, and then fell on his butt and on his back. So he got hurt on a great fielding play. And he got the out. He would've been really upset if he hadn't gotten the out.

He also hurt his calf. But let me tell you what: he pitched when a lot of guys wouldn't have pitched. He still had a 16-6 record and he was second in the league in earned run average. He pitched under 200 innings, but as a team we only had three complete games the whole season even though we had 15 shutouts.

That's when the bullpen came into play. It was such an effective weapon. We had our ducks in order and pretty much if we went six innings and had the lead, there was a real good chance we were going to win. That doesn't mean we wanted our starters to only go six, but when you have a bullpen like we had, you have that luxury. It doesn't happen every year. We may go in this season looking for Maddux to go eight or nine next year, as opposed to six or seven.

In Game 4, there were some bloop hits and a ball hit into the gap off Glavine. And before you know it, we're down. Once again, he felt strong. It was very similar to his first outing. The change of speeds wasn't there.

After the game, there was a lot of talk on the radio that Glavine was washed up. Come on. There was talk in '92 when we started him in the first game of the World Series because

Pittsburgh had knocked him out in the NLCS. My answer to that was: what's wrong with starting a 20-game winner in the first game of the World Series? And what's wrong with starting a pitcher with 18 wins in the first game of the playoffs?

We lost Game 5 3-1. In the ninth, we had runners at the corners with nobody out and couldn't get the runs in. That was a frustrating game because we had opportunities to win. Nobody played bad in that series. The Giants played good and we played good. Nobody butchered anything. It was just two good teams, two solid teams, playing the game of baseball the way it should be played.

MAD DOG RISING

Maddux won 16 games in 2002. He is the first pitcher since Cy Young to win at least 15 games in 15 different seasons. That one ranks high on the list, it's probably his number one accomplishment in the game. That means you're real good over a long period of time.

You want to talk consistency? How about 13 Gold Glove Awards over the last 13 seasons? Maddux is like a hockey goalie out there. He's the greatest-fielding pitcher I've ever seen, bar none. Smoltz is in that category. And Glavine. They are all great pitchers and great fielders. They're great bunters; they can put the ball in play if you need them to. And they're great base runners.

Maddux told me that before he retires he wants to play in the outfield one inning. Will I let him? I don't have a say in it. But Bobby and I might look at one another some day and

WALKING TO THE BULLPEN WITH MADDUX.

then tell him, "Go on, get out there." That's the least we can do for him.

TEACHING TRADITION

Going into the 2003 season, you know Glavine's not there for the first time and you know that Millwood's not there and Remlinger's not there and Hammond's not there and Ligtenberg's not there and Spoony's not there and Mossy's not there. That's a lot. By the same token, Mike Hampton *is* here. Russ Ortiz is here. Paul Byrd is here. Jason Marquis is here.

Then there's the big man down at the end, Smoltzie. It isn't like you're starting out with nothing.

As a matter of fact, the rotation to me sounds pretty darned good. The potential to have a really good rotation is certainly staring us in the face.

People have asked if this season will be my greatest challenge as pitching coach. No. The biggest challenge was the first full year, 1991. I look at every year as a big challenge. I don't look at one as bigger than the other. All I look at is how my pitching staff is shaping up, and I work off that.

In the end, it all goes back to your rotation. How much do you expose your bullpen? Your rotation allows you to use your bullpen in a more effective way. And not having a good rotation can put your bullpen in a shambles. The emphasis always gets back to starting pitching and then you work off of that. If the rotation is taking you deep into the game, then you're in good shape. The rotation will dictate how much you expose your bullpen, either to vulnerability or to being really good. The last two years, the bullpen has been extremely outstanding. They are the best bullpens we've ever had.

I've never thought we had bad bullpens. The bullpen got a bad rap over the years because of the extreme excellence of the starting rotation. Pena and Stanton and McMichael and Ligtenberg and Wohlers and Rocker and Rudy and Remlinger … we've had good bullpens. They just haven't had any room for error. Every mistake was magnified because we were winning. And when we did lose, the first question was always: Who came in to relieve?

One thing you have to think about is there is a history and a tradition of winning in Atlanta. Professional sports is played to win and it's played to set a standard of excellence. If you come here from another team, you've got to be able to handle that. I've seen a lot of pitchers who can win on a second division club; on a first division club, they can't do it. Or a lot of pitchers who can pitch the sixth or seventh inning, and can't pitch the eighth or ninth.

Then you see pitchers who are good regardless of what inning they pitch. You're getting back to the make-up of the individual. Who wants more responsibility? Who's satisfied with what they've got? Who really wants no part of something? And that's an individual thing.

Fond Adieu

Of course, we're going to miss Tommy Glavine. And Millwood, who was traded to Philadelphia. He came to us as a young pitcher, hard working and very dedicated. A country hardball guy who was all business. No bull, loves to win, loves to compete. And what Kevin did, he took advantage of what was in that dugout. The manager, the pitching coach, and then Maddux, Glavine and Smoltz. And he picked their brains—listened and watched and learned. And he was not intimidated by it at all.

We've run some younger starting pitchers through here who couldn't handle that part of it. They'd say we wanted them to pitch like Glavine or Maddux or Smoltz. We didn't want them to pitch like them. We wanted them to watch how they prepare and how they dedicate themselves and their consistency in that work ethic, and how that thought process helped them to be successful.

And Kevin is that way. That's one of the main reasons he's had success. Like last season, he brought the two-seam fastball back on the corner, ala Greg Maddux. He worked on it and worked on it and then when he broke it out, he became even better.

He had some shoulder problems and he added a lot of motion to protect the shoulder. And then once his shoulder didn't hurt, he still had the extra motions. So we were able to cut down and eliminate some wasted motion. Kevin's a very coachable guy, very well liked and very professional. I hate to see him go.

You knew the numbers didn't add up in terms of what our payroll has to be this season. I was hoping against hope that it would be one of the new guys who would go. There'll be a close relationship with them, too. It's just that when you part ways with a Glavine and a Millwood, you're not only parting ways with pitchers who are class acts and good pitchers but good people who have been major contributors to your career and to your success. So you get emotionally attached.

With Maddux, I just kept hoping he would sign. Once again, I was wrong. I thought he would probably leave. That's just the gut feeling I was getting. I sure was a happy camper when I heard he was staying. He'll lead the pitching staff because he is the Number One guy. Then everything else falls into place with the two, three and four holes—Hampton, Ortiz and Byrd. You have to keep your ducks in order with the starters, just like you do in the bullpen to get to Smoltzie. If you start moving guys up to slots where they don't belong, it becomes a little more difficult. So it was a great thing for the Braves to have Maddux return.

One thing all of our pitchers have had in common is a lot of talk about pitching. They all love to talk about pitching, and they're very serious about it. You get an exchange of ideas that is very important. And everybody wants to pick Maddux's brain. I still do, for sure. I've never met anybody who can talk as intelligently about pitching as Greg Maddux. I don't care who it is.

We'll have almost an entirely new pitching staff who will learn the program here. We have a good track record, so it isn't hard to sell. Once again, being able to hear about it from the pitchers who actually do it makes a big difference. There are going to be some new guys here this year, and they're going to have to have a lot of conversations with Maddux and Smoltz. And then Smoltzie will take it down to the bullpen. You have Bobby Dews coaching the bullpen, who understands everything we try to do and will reinforce it all. Or he'll talk it and Smoltzie reinforces it.

I've been taught over the years what works. I had a farm director call me not long ago, and he wanted me to help him out with his pitching. So I went into what we do here. In the middle of the conversation he said, "Well, you can't do that." I thought, well, you're just wasting a phone call. Personally, I don't care what anybody else does. What I care about is the Atlanta Braves pitchers.

SPRING TRAINING

Someone asked me in the off season if I'd watched any film on Mike Hampton. He seemed shocked that I hadn't. I don't need to. I'll watch him throw. I'll exchange ideas with him. Get his thoughts. And then work off of that. Everyone talks about how his career went sour in Colorado. I'm not really concerned about Hampton. He'll be our number two starter and I'm really looking forward to working with him. I've got a plan for sinkers and change-ups down and away. And just getting him out of Coors Field will help. Our challenge will be to get him back on top of his game and pitch a lot of innings.

I'll work it the same way with Russ Ortiz and Paul Byrd. I'll familiarize myself with them. And then work off that. You get their ideas first. Then whatever adjustments they make, you make them think it's their idea.

After we picked up Byrd, I read in the paper where he said, "I feel like I dropped the ball when I was here the first time, and Leo and I butted heads." I had to laugh because it was true. We'd had Byrd in '97 and '98. He'd never had success before coming to us, and when pitchers haven't had much success, you have a game plan for them to follow that's already proven to be very successful with other pitchers. And if they don't like to use it, it does kind of bother you a little bit. Especially when they're not succeeding. I think in the case of Paul Byrd, now that he's had some success I'm going to let him go ahead and express himself about how he wants to go about pitching. And go from there. In Birdman's case, I think he's a better pitcher now. Therefore, I'll be more open to his ideas. By the same token, he should be more open to mine.

These new guys can see the track record here. So selling them on the program shouldn't be difficult. I don't even worry about that; I just go about it. I know what Ortiz can do. I've seen what Hampton can do. I've seen what Byrd can do, as far as being a little more unorthodox. And I can see Marquis maturing.

You've just got to have your top guy in place. And who better than Greg Maddux?

EXTRA INNINGS:
GOING DOWN AND AWAY

Of course, the one thing I'm known for is when they see me on TV in the dugout and I'm rocking back and forth. And everybody wants to know the same thing: why? I don't know. My mom said I'd sit in my high chair when I was a baby, and I'd rock and beat my head against the wall. As I grew up, it never stopped. When I was pitching, I rocked all the time. And now I do it as a coach. I really don't know when I'm doing it half the time.

It's a soothing thing. And when I'm rocking, my wheels are turning. I rock a lot at a Notre Dame football game. It's what happens when you're in a high-intensity situation. And that's my way of getting through it.

One time we were playing the Phillies when Jim Fregosi was their manager. I looked over in the dugout and the whole team was rocking. And Fregosi peeked around the corner and gave me the "You're crazy" sign, pointing his finger at his head and rolling it over. Robbie Thompson would do it on the on-deck circle—he'd look over at me and start rocking. Some of the Cubs guys would do the same thing. It's been mimicked quite a bit, which I kind of like. It's become my signature.

One of the local radio stations did a song called "Rockin' Leo." It was based on "Rockin' Robin." I've got a tape of it. It goes: "He rocks in the dugout all night long / Hoping that his pitchers will stay real strong / There's Maddux, Glavine, Smoltz and Avery, too / Hoping his pitchers will stay strong the whole year through / Rockin' Leo, rock, rock / Go rockin' Leo / the Braves are gonna win tonight."

The first time I heard that, I was driving down the interstate to the Chop Shop. We were in the World Series, and it came on the radio. And I was so pumped. I looked down and I was going 90 mph down I-75.

Oh, by the way, it was done by the Shower Stall Singers.

CAMP LEO

At the first of every February, we have what's become known as "Camp Leo." I never called it that; I always called it the "early throwing program." But the press started calling it "Camp Leo," and it's stuck. It started when I got together with Bobby Cox and John Schuerholz and talked about bringing in some pitchers for early workouts before spring training. We were in the West Division at the time, and I'd turn on the TV and see the Dodgers working out at Chez Ravine.

They were going to be our main competition in the West; they were a powerhouse at the time and we were in last place.

So we thought it would be a great idea to bring in our top 12 or 13 guys for some early pitching sessions and get a head start on spring training.

My idea was to get the pitchers in there early and start developing a rapport with them. I also thought it would help them get through the first parts of spring training without any stiffness, which helps keep your pitchers healthy. You're also in a very relaxed atmosphere; guys are in the clubhouse shooting the bull. It's totally voluntary, and it just seemed to go off real well. It's become a tradition now.

All the pitchers love it. And now if you're a pitcher, you want to be the one picked to come in and do Camp Leo. Especially if you're a young pitcher trying to make the staff. What helped establish Camp Leo was that Glavine was always the first one on the mound. And the one who got on the mound the most. Smoltz was always there when he was supposed to be there. And Maddux's first year, he was there.

I can get those pitchers on the mound six or seven times prior to going down to spring training. We always hold the camp beginning with the first Monday of February. We report to spring training two weeks later. It can get cold in Atlanta in February, but we get outside a lot. If you go down to the visitors' bullpen at Turner Field and the sun's shining, it's great. In fact, that's where Darren Holmes was signed in 2002. There are some camps where we don't get outside at all; we've got indoor mounds and indoor tunnels, so it's no big deal.

We're really not looking to make discoveries, although that's how we spotted Holmes and Chris Hammond. What I'm trying to do is re-familiarize myself with the veteran pitchers again and then familiarize myself with some of the younger pitchers we may be counting on during the season. The bottom line is it's geared to the pitchers' health, getting them throwing ahead of spring training.

It's amazing. I've been with Smoltzie 13 years and I had Tommy for 12. And yet I had to restart it all over again whenever they started throwing. Their mechanics would be off. Usually, I have them pitch two days and then take one off. All we do is get on the mound and get some touch on the pitches. It's pretty much what we do in between starts in the regular season.

AIN'T SUPERSTITIOUS

Am I superstitious? Oh yeah. There are certain ways I'll drive to the park. I know if I turn right out of this condo complex, it's a longer drive. But we give up fewer runs when I take a right rather than go left. I wore a certain Notre Dame T-shirt under my uniform every time Glavine pitched. I don't know what I'm going to do this year. I'm not going to wear it when he pitches, that's for sure.

In '93 we hit a hot streak when I wore a T-shirt from the Notre Dame-Miami University game: "Catholics vs. Convicts." I wore it so much it fell apart. But it worked. We went 54-19.

THE SEVEN-SECOND RULE

Mad Dog has this way of recognizing what a hitter is trying to do against him. He's one of the very few pitchers I've ever been around who can recognize something *before* the fact, not after the fact. He studies the game and he watches film.

He doesn't watch film of himself; he watches the players he's going to face. He studies the game. He can sit on the bench during a game and predict things that are going to happen with the other team.

One time when he was with the Cubs, he called the pitches for his own teammate. The pitcher asked him to call the game, so he'd look into the dugout and Mad Dog would give him the signal for the pitch.

To show how you become a smart coach, Maddux was pitching in a ballgame and was up by one run. There were runners on second and third, two outs, and a short pop fly to left. Nobody could find the ball. All of a sudden, Ryan Klesko came diving in from left field and made the catch. Maddux came in and he was pretty irate, to say the least. I said, "Take it easy, we made the play."

"Look, Leo," he says, "That ball was in the air seven seconds."

I looked at him with this puzzled look. "What?"

"Any time the ball is in the air for seven seconds, it's an easy catch," he said. "Four seconds is a dive, and three seconds is a base hit in fair territory."

I just kept staring at him with my mouth open. "Well, I knew that!" I finally said. And I couldn't keep a straight face. I went, holy hell! But if you think about it, he was right.

"So it shouldn't be that tough," he said. "Let's go!"

We ended up winning the game. Dave Campbell of ESPN was scouting us for a TV game. The next day he was in the dugout trading jokes and stuff and he goes, "Hey, Leo, I saw Mad Dog coming in ranting and raving the other night. But he didn't give up a run."

I said, "My God, Dave, the ball was in the air for seven seconds!" He looked at me the same way I'd looked at Mad Dog. I said, "Well, seven seconds is an easy catch, four seconds is a diving catch and three seconds is a base hit in fair territory."

"How in the hell do you know that?"

I shrugged. "It's just kind of common knowledge among us pitching coaches. Hey, that's why I'm not just another pretty face in the crowd."

And sure as hell, our "seven-second rule" surfaced on TV. Then a couple of weeks later, I even heard Tim McCarver say, "The Braves believe that if the ball is in the air for seven seconds ..."

We had a lot of fun with that. And to this day, I've never told anybody any different. And it went around the world.

DEFENSIVELY SPEAKING

Mad Dog holds himself to a high standard when it comes to defense. I've never seen a guy anticipate like Maddux. I've seen him break left off the mound, break right, break forward, leap high in the air, pick balls off his shoes and off his shins, off his shoulders, off his elbows. I remember one time in San Diego, he got hit in the elbow and I thought his career was over. It hit him smack on his pitching elbow. We thought it was broke. He came off the mound and didn't miss a start. He got hit on his foot in spring training and busted his toe. Got hit on the shin. Everything else he can get his glove on, the hitter's out. I've seen pitchers react after contact was made; he's almost doing it beforehand.

When we go to spring training, we have our PFP drills, pitchers' fielding practice. And Maddux is always the leader of his group; he gets on guys about doing it right. Smoltz and Glavine are the other two leaders. If you have Greg Maddux leading the way on fielding practice, what choice do the others have except to follow suit? They have none. And he lets them know about it.

You can take every pitcher in the game of baseball and hit them a million ground balls, and it's not going to matter. Fielding that position is just reaction and athleticism and anticipation. Sure, you have to practice the fundamentals. But when they practice, they know the ball's coming to them. The bottom line on shots back to the mound is reaction.

I've never seen a guy make better plays on balls back up the box than Maddux. I've never see a guy make plays on bunts along the lines that are impossible to pick up and throw to first base than Smoltz. A bunt down the third base line, he'll go get it and throw to first off balance or falling on his butt and make an accurate throw.

Maddux stops a ton of base hits going up the middle. There are times when he'll tell our infielders at times to shade somebody toward the hole; he'll tell them he has the middle. That if it goes up the middle and he doesn't catch it, then the batter deserves a base hit.

That's why he has 13 Gold Glove Awards. And counting.

BEST OF AN ERA

Here's an amazing stat about Mad Dog. Sandy Koufax has the greatest ERA over an entire decade, 2.36 in the '60s, in the entire history of baseball. Greg Maddux is second, a 2.54 ERA in the '90s.

Sandy Koufax over a six- or seven-year period was the greatest pitcher the game has ever seen. You look at his numbers and laugh because you're never going to see anything like that again. You look at Maddux's numbers, you're not going to see that again either.

It was a different style, a different era. But in Maddux's era—the era of the long ball and the offense and the small ballparks and juiced-up balls and juiced-up bats and home run records being broken—when you put that 2.54 ERA in perspective it is absolutely unbelievable. Just imagine what he would have done had he pitched in Koufax's era.

NO SWEAT

Glavine's the best hot-weather pitcher I've ever seen. He can go and go and go and not have the fatigue factor set in. In the middle of the season, when it's a hundred degrees out and it's a day game, Bobby and I will look at one another and say, "Man, it's hot today; we'd better have our pen ready."

Then you look at Glavine and say, "Well, let's remember one thing: we've got the best hot-weather pitcher in the game. That's Tom Glavine."

He may get tired, but you don't see it. He doesn't sweat much. If he tells you he's tired, you better listen. Because I've seen him go out there and throw 130 pitches in 100-degree weather and say he's fine. And, really, it's the mental part, not the actual delivery of the pitches, that makes you tired when you're pitching an important game.

GETTING HIT

There was an incident in '93 where we were playing Cincinnati; Tim Belcher hit Deion Sanders. There was the feeling with some of the players that it was intentional. Marvin Freeman was on the mound for us, and he didn't return the favor when Belcher came up to bat the next inning. Terry Pendleton was playing third, and he walked off the field in the middle of the inning. Walked off and never came back. We were all wondering what the hell was going on. That was Terry's way of showing that hey, you've got to stick up for your guys.

They asked Marvin about it after the game, and he responded with one of the greatest lines from any pitcher I've ever been around. They asked Marvin what he thought when he saw his third baseman walking off the field? And Marvin told the reporters, "Well, I guess he thought my stuff was so good that we didn't need a third baseman." That was an awesome answer.

We were in Tampa one time. They had been trying to pitch everybody inside, and they hit Galarraga a couple of times. Then they hit Walt Weiss. So Mad Dog was heading out for the eighth inning and said, "Well, I gotta do something." He turned to Walt and said, "Walt, you want me to do something?"

And Walt said, "Yup."

The pitcher was slated to lead off the next inning. Instead, they pinch hit and it was Jose Canseco. I kind of knew Mad Dog was going to drill the first guy up. I looked out there and I went, oh, hell, it's Canseco. He hit him in the knee. Canseco kind of gave him a grin and walked on down to first. Because Canseco knew what was going on. We'd been getting drilled like crazy and hadn't done anything.

Here's the difference. Maddux got the next guy to hit into a double play. He had a one-run lead in the eighth inning, and it was the tying run he'd hit in the knee. From there, he retired the side. We were all in the dugout and Mad Dog was shaking. I said, "What's the matter, Mad Dog?"

He said, "That guy could have killed me; he could have broke me in two. Look at my hands. They're shaking."

Chipper Jones walked over and said, "Don't worry, I would have gotten there before he did."

And Brian Jordan came in from right field and said, "I gotta hand it to ya, Doggie, you picked the biggest son of a gun in the park to hit."

Another time, Maddux tried to get inside on McGwire. He wasn't trying to hit him. He was just trying to back him up because McGwire was hanging out over the right side of the plate. So Maddux hit him. McGwire went down to first base, and Mad Dog went over to first base, too. And I thought, what in the hell is he doing? He's gonna get killed. He came back to the mound and got the next guy out. I asked him, "What were you doing going over to first base?"

He said, "I just went over to ask him if that hurt at all."

"What'd he say?"

"No." Maddux gave his head a little shake. "Took my best ball, too."

GLAV VS. MURPH

We were playing Philly in '91 when one of their pitchers hit Otis Nixon. Again, it seemed intentional. Glavine's pitching and who's the first batter up in the next inning? Dale Murphy. Glavine and Murphy had played together. Everybody adores Murphy. He was an icon in Atlanta.

Glavine feels obligated. So he tries to hit Murph with something like a 65 mph change-up. Glavine threw three more lollipops at him and missed every time. And everybody was just looking at each other. Murphy was looking at him like "What are you doing?" And Glavine was shrugging and the umpire looked puzzled. After the fourth pitch, he tossed Glavine out of the game. Tommy wanted to protect his teammate, but he just couldn't hit Dale Murphy.

In the 12 years I've been pitching coach here, we've always led the league in the smallest number of hit batsmen. We feel that's reserved for mediocre staffs. If somebody has to hit somebody because the guy hit a home run off of him, then you're not a very good pitcher. Not if you have to resort to something like that. I think it's idiotic. Now, if you're protecting a teammate or the circumstance makes it obvious, you have that inner baseball circle that thinks, okay, you've got to protect your guy. But to just hit guys to be a macho man out there or because you can't get a guy out, to me that's ridiculous.

Fun with the Cheering Gallery

Mad Dog has a nasty sense of humor. He can say the raunchiest stuff. And it's just funny as hell because he has that innocent-sounding schoolboy voice. One year, we were at Wrigley and standing there getting ready for the National Anthem. They were hard on Mad Dog at Wrigley. You heard this loud cry out of the bleachers: "Hey, Maddux, you suck!" And then there was a pause. "You do, too, Mazzone."

Mad Dog looks at me and goes, "Hey, welcome to the club, Coach!"

Then Mad Dog went out and threw a shutout.

The Routine

On game day, I get to the clubhouse between one and two o'clock for a night game, and at nine in the morning for a day game. I've tried over the years to cut it down a little bit. But you can't do it. You try. You say, well, this year I'm not going to go to the park as early as I normally would. But it never happens.

First, I run on the treadmill to clear my brain. I feel I can think better after exercising. And then I get ready for the day's work. The first game of every series, the whole team gathers. It's not broken down in individual groups. Bobby calls the meeting and tells me to go over the hitters. Then you have your hitting instructor go over their pitchers. I like the way Bobby does it. Because of the manager's presence in those meetings, there's a lot higher attention span.

In those meetings, you have to be very careful as you read the advance reports and prepare them. In the 12 years that I've been here, I've never told a pitcher you *can't* throw a certain pitch.

Our philosophy is to be on the attack. You can either go out in a prevent defense or be in an offensive mode and on the attack. And we're always saying: be on the attack. Every report you get says a guy is a first-ball, fastball hitter. What are you supposed to do? Not throw a fastball on the first pitch? We're going to throw a fastball on the first pitch, down and away, and let the batter get himself out. If he takes it, it's strike one. If he hits it, it's a groundball out.

Then you have your sessions on the side for the pitchers. What we call getting the dust off, getting ready for their next starts. But the side sessions stay consistent as far as the effort, the amount of time. It doesn't change regardless of the performance in the previous start. It goes about 10 minutes for each pitcher.

Then we bring over the relievers. I take a poll every day of the relievers, asking whether they are good to go. I have that ready for Bobby, so that we can exchange ideas on how many relievers will be available that day and who needs a breather. It's all predetermined before the game starts.

You create a program for your relievers just like your starters to make sure that all 11 or 12 get the same amount of attention. It gives the reliever the opportunity to work with the pitching coach, and you always tell that reliever that he's preparing for that night's game. Any pitcher who's come over and said he needs to throw more, I've never said no. I'm always encouraging them to throw.

Smoltzie used to throw the day before he started. Tommy too. When I got here in 1990, I told Glavine what we were going to do in the throwing program. He said, "Well, I'll meet you here at the park at two o'clock."

I said, "What goes on at two o'clock?"

"Well, that's when I'm gonna throw," he said.

"What do you do after that?"

"Hang out," he said.

"Well, here's what we're gonna do," I said. "What time do the pitchers hit?"

"4:55."

"What time are they done?"

"5:10."

"Okay," I said. "Meet me in the bullpen at 5:11. That's when we're gonna throw. Because hitters will be taking batting practice, and the infielders will be taking ground balls and outfielders will be taking fly balls. So that's when we're going to do our work in the bullpen. And then when our time is up and we leave the field, we'll all be leaving the field together."

In the past, pitchers would try to sneak out of practice, go hang out in the outfield and shag fly balls. What I wanted to do was try to organize the time in a fashion that worked with the entire team and wouldn't have pitchers as a separate entity. That's basically what the day consists of. And it's every single day of the season.

THE MEDICINE BAG

There's an old bag that I use to carry the baseballs down to the bullpen before the game. If you see me before a game, I'll have that bag. I got it in '91. They tried to put a new bag in my locker the next year, and I said, "Forget it." You can't change it. A lot of the other pitching coaches are always kidding me: There goes Leo with his bag; he's got his firm grip, his razor blades and his sandpaper in that thing and he ain't gonna let nobody look in that bag.

You'd be amazed at what's in that bag sometimes. Sometimes those guys will put a weighted ball in there. And you pick it up, and it'll barely come up and you think: either it's getting heavier, or else I'm getting weaker as I get older.

It's filthy now. The blue canvas has turned to rosin. But that just makes the balls feel better.

IN RELIEF

If a reliever goes more than two days without getting into a game, I try to really insist that they come over to a side session and throw a little bit. Of course, if you're being used a lot, you're not going to do it. If you're winning and you have 11 pitchers, six or seven of them are doing most of the pitching. And I'm hoping every day that I have pitchers come in and complain that they're not getting enough work. Because if everybody's getting to pitch, that means something's not right at the front part of that staff.

Steve Bedrosian used to complain all the time. Bedrock, even though he was on the downside of his career, added so much to our pitching staff as far as what we were all about.

Tremendous competitor. Won the Cy Young in '87 when he was the closer in Philly. In '95, he wasn't getting into very many games. He'd wait on me down in the pen: "I haven't pitched in six days."

And I'd look at him and say, "I know that, Rock. Let's throw a little bit to get ready for tonight."

He'd say, "I'm going to air it out. Don't look like I'm gonna get in."

So we'd go back and forth a little bit and he'd rev it up a little, and then he was fine. You always run into that: How come I'm not pitching? Well, you tell them that the starters are going great right now, that they're taking us right to our closer. Or that they're going nine. You let them sound off, and then you explain to them why they aren't pitching.

Of course, you have to explain to a couple of pitchers that they aren't pitching because they haven't pitched well when called upon. You tell them that if they want to get into a few more games, then get a few three-up and three-down innings when the manager calls them in. And then he'll start to ride the hot hand. It's not that difficult to figure out.

WHEN ENOUGH'S ENOUGH

You hear a lot about pitchers who never tell their pitching coach or manager that they're tired. They're afraid they'll be marked as someone who won't go the distance. We have the opposite philosophy in Atlanta. We take a poll of our pitchers before every game to find out how they're feeling. We want them to feel a part of it. We want them to know that we're not going to think something bad about them if they say they can't go. It takes time to build that trust.

When John Burkett was first here, he started a game and got into the sixth inning. I asked him, "Do you have another one in you, or are you done?" And he looked at me with this funny look on his face. And I said, "Look, if you're okay, you're going to hit. And if you're not, we'll pinch hit for you. But I need to know something." He still didn't say a word. So I said, "Why do you have that look on your face?"

"Because nobody's ever asked me that before," he said. "They've always *told me* when I'm in or out."

We also do that with our relievers. We used to give Rocker a day or two off. We'd go to him and say, you're not pitching today. There are games when a reliever said, I'm ready to go, even when he's been in two or three games in a row. If he says he's ready to roll and gives me a thumbs-up, okay. Then there are guys who pitch two games and say they're hanging and need a breather, so you adjust the game plan and go with that. And I think pitchers appreciate that.

It's silly to punish honesty. At the same time, I'm always jabbing the starters: "Hey, don't be afraid to get a complete game."

Of course, Mad Dog comes back and says, "Complete games are overrated."

Complete games have dropped way down and it's just the evolution of baseball. You have the setup man. But I still preach that you start a game to go nine, not six. I think "quality starts" is a bad stat. It goes back to the old school of thinking. Starting pitchers going nine. The reason I preach it all the time is that I don't want them thinking that if they've gone six, they've done their job.

BOBBY DEWS

The bullpen coach is very important, and I think it's a huge mistake if he's a former pitcher. You wind up creating problems that need not be there. As the pitching coach, you want things done a certain way after you've exchanged ideas with the pitcher. If the pitcher is not having success, he's going to seek out somebody else. And if that somebody else tells him what he wants to hear, instead of telling him the truth, then you have a problem.

Bobby Dews and I work great together. We talk every day. He comes down and watches me work with their mechanics, and he does a great job of following suit. Bobby also is a sounding board, to sit down there and listen to the pitchers. He's great at that, too. He has a tremendous sense of humor and a great knowledge of the game. He makes sure there's no division there, that he and I are working together as one. He'll volunteer to me that a guy had a funny look on his face warming up. He lets me know which guys are throwing great, or whose attitudes are good, or whose attitudes might not be good.

WALK, DON'T RUN

I've never gotten on pitchers for walks in my career. On the other hand, we've always led the league in fewest number of hit batsmen and fewest walks. A pitcher walks a guy or two, right? You go out to the mound. The first thing you *can't* say is, "Come on, man, throw the ball over the plate." They're going to look at you and say, "No shit."

What I try to do when I go out there is say, "Look, those hitters are gone. Don't give in to the strike zone. This is about making pitches, trying to execute a good pitch. So forget about walks. And don't throw one down the middle just because you walked a guy. I'd rather you be off the plate a little than give up a three-run bomb."

So once again, you take the emphasis off giving up bases on balls and continue to try to make good pitches.

A BONDS FIB

If you were to ask me now how to get Barry Bonds out, I couldn't tell you. He was great back in '91 and '92; he's the greatest now. When you're talking about great hitters like McGwire and Sammy Sosa and Darryl Strawberry, we've always felt there were holes to go to and ways to get them out. We always felt that if we executed our pitch, we were going to get them out. A guy like Bonds, you can execute the pitch and still not get him out

I remember one time, Bonds told Maddux, "If you pitch to me, I won't steal second. But if you walk me, I'm gonna steal."

We were playing the Giants in postseason. He got a base hit, then he stole second base. Maddux came into the dugout and said, "Well, I guess this is playoff time ... because he *lied* to me!"

THE GREAT HITTERS

Tony Gwynn stands out, of course. Our strategy with Tony Gwynn was to give him a single to left because he could do more damage on a mistake inside. There are certain hitters that if they get a single then that's fine. We had a game in Houston one time where Jeff Bagwell got four hits. We won the game. A sportswriter asked me, "What are you going to do to stop Bagwell?"

And I said, "We did."

He goes, "Well, he got four hits."

I said, "Yeah, and they were all singles."

We don't mind giving up a solo home run to Bonds. I always tell pitchers, you can give up four solo home runs in a game and still go nine. But that one three-runner's going to get you an early exit. Mercker was pitching one time in Cincinnati, and he gave up three solo homers in the seventh inning. He said, "I think I'm carrying your theory a little too far." But we were in the game, down three to nothing.

A guy who's been a thorn in our sides all these years is Eric Young. We have a difficult time getting him out. If you made a mistake to Will Clark, you didn't get away with it. There are some hitters, you can throw it down the middle and pop them up. The worst that happened to us in that division series we lost to the Cardinals in 2000 was Mark McGwire being hurt. And that's nothing against McGwire, for sure. But Will Clark was his replacement. He was playing every day, and he's been a big thorn in our sides for a long time. By the same token, the biggest out of the '93 season was when Glavine got Will Clark to hit into that double play in that big series out in St. Louis with the bases loaded and one out. Tommy got him to roll over on a change-up. And we took off and won that series from there and then caught the Giants in the great pennant race of '93.

One day, I went out and watched Tony Gwynn take batting practice. I do that all the time, and I count the balls they hit that would be hits in a game. I saw Tony Gwynn go eight for eight. I saw him spray the balls, starting in left field, and then methodically going to every part of the park, from left to right.

Another thing on Tony Gwynn: you didn't want anyone on base when he was up because they would hit and run. And if the second baseman covered, he could hit it right in the hole that was vacated. If the shortstop covered, he could smack it through that hole. So Bobby had the infielders hold their ground on the hit-and-run when Gwynn was at bat. That's something special.

Tony didn't want to walk. So you'd think, "Don't throw him a strike." But he could hit *anything*. Tommy Glavine had so-so success against Gwynn. One time they asked him how he planned to pitch to Gwynn. Tommy said he was going to throw it right down the middle and hope Gwynn didn't get a hit.

SMOLTZIE'S SECRET

As beautiful as it is, Smoltzie doesn't throw the curve any more. He's fastball, slider and split. But if you had ten scouts in the stands, a lot of them would call his slider a short curveball. His slider breaks more than your average slider, and it has a curveball tilt on it. The emergence of his split-finger really made a difference with him. It goes on a line, then just dips down. There's not a pitch invented that he can't throw.

I know what he's gone through, physically, to be where he is today. I know what a lot of those guys have gone through, going to the post when they're not feeling good. Smoltz has gone through a lot, through a lot of pain. He pitched with it for quite some time. I've seen Maddux pitch with it. And Glavine and Avery and Millwood. It's no accident why those guys are good, and it's no accident why they do what they do. Besides the physical talent, they have a strong competitive mentality.

THE DREAM JOB

The best thing about my job is there aren't a whole lot of people in the world who can say they can't wait to go to work. The adrenaline starts to flow in spring training and you get this gleam in your eye. There's the excitement that I always have, that I've had ever since I was nine years old and pitching Little League games. That has never faded whatsoever.

I've appreciated this run every single year. It kind of boggles your mind to look back over the last 12 years and all the accomplishments we've achieved. The number of wins, being in the pennant race every year, and having the opportunity to go to the World Series. Being in five of them. It's unprecedented in the history of professional sports. If you take away that extra tier of playoffs or if you went straight into the

World Series like they did in the old days, there would be a lot more World Series wins.

You hear some complaints here and there about how we've *only* won one World Series. I think that's a joke. Winning over the long haul and doing what we've done and accomplishing what we've accomplished, we take a back seat to nobody. No organization, no league. I truly believe that with TBS, we are America's Team. Make no mistake about it. You'll get some arguments from the Yankees. But the Yankees only.

If we'd won one more World Series, I don't think we'd have to sit here and defend ourselves. And we shouldn't have to anyway. But that's the world of professional sports.

When it's all said and done, when we're not here any more doing this year in and year out, I think it will be appreciated a whole heckuva lot more by people than it is now.

People have the tendency to get spoiled. But I would much rather spoil them by winning than to be one of those organizations that talks about trying to get to .500 or trying to get into the postseason for the first time.

When you give yourself the opportunity to go to the playoffs 12 years in a row, the other teams keep changing. Pittsburgh was in the playoffs for two years. Philly for one year. Florida, one year. San Diego. The Mets. Dodgers. The Cubs. All one year. The Braves being there 12 years running is one of the most remarkable feats in the history of sports. Come on. It's great just to have the opportunity to be knocked off. It's always a great feeling to know you're one of only a few teams left playing after the regular season is over.

You never expect to be there. You treat every season as a new season, where you start from the beginning. Naturally, your goal is to get to the World Series and win it. But you start every season fresh. Because the personnel changes. Other clubs change. So you start anew and then work toward your goal. You can't think, well, just because we're the Braves we're going to the postseason. It takes a lot of hard work. It takes a lot of thought. It takes a lot of talent. You can't take anything for granted.

What you want to do is give yourself the opportunity to be in the pennant race. After that, you go with it.

We've had four World Series decided in the final game by one run. That's a bloop hit, a bounce, a pitch. There's luck involved in professional sports. But the better you are, the more luck you have. You make your own luck for the most part. And we're pretty damned good at that.

Since the run is still going on, it's hard to put the 12 years in perspective. It still kind of blows your mind. You still go, wow! What a tremendous thing we've done. We're going to be in baseball history. We'll be talked about for a long, long, long time. And it's still going on. We're not putting it to rest just yet.

FINAL PITCH:
ODE TO JOHNNY

Whitey Ford was small in stature, and early in his career, the Yankees thought they had to give him more rest than the other pitchers. They thought he'd wear down over the course of a season because he was small, so they would have him skip starts against lesser teams. They'd pitch him in the big games because he was "the chairman of the board," and he always rose to the occasion. But he'd only win 12 or 14 games a year.

Johnny Sain got there and began to pitch him every four days. Whitey Ford won 25-4 and won Cy Youngs because Johnny didn't follow the preconceived notions about Ford's size.

You hear me say that great pitchers make for good pitching coaches, and good pitching coaches don't mess up great pitchers. Denny McClain was already a 20-game winner when Johnny Sain got to Detroit. Well, Denny McClain then became a 30-game winner. Greg Maddux was already a great pitcher when he got to Atlanta. No question, he'd already won a Cy Young. He didn't get worse. He won three more Cy Youngs. So maybe he got a little better.

Look at some of the young pitchers Sain worked with. You had a guy like Ralph Terry, who became a 20-game winner. Never had much success anyplace else. You can look at some of the pitchers who had success here in Atlanta, and then didn't have it any place else. There's a correlation there. That's because I basically do what Sain did in terms of the teachings, the approach, the philosophies. All the things you've seen happen with Braves pitching over the last 12 years, that's Johnny Sain carried forward with me doing a little tweaking here and there.

I can only imagine my career had I encountered Johnny when I was still pitching. It would have made a huge difference. If Sain had taught me, I certainly would have changed speeds a lot more, instead of trying to pound my way through. And I wouldn't try to go over 100 percent effort. Everything that I teach now, everything I try to prevent, I used to do myself: I'd try to throw it harder than I could, I'd try to throw a breaking ball better than I could, I'd try to make the perfect pitch every time. I was a good pitcher. I lasted 10 years in the minor leagues. A little more change of speed would have sure as hell helped. A little less blind aggressiveness, too.

I worked hard. Nobody worked harder than me. But my ability to work smart maybe wasn't quite up to par with what I needed to have done in order to pitch in the big leagues.

Johnny Sain influenced so many people. Jim Kaat was broadcasting Yankee games, and he'd always talk to me when we went to Yankee Stadium. He'd call out, "Hey Leo! Throw, turn and pull." That's how Johnny Sain taught you to throw the breaking stuff, the same way I taught Smoltzie.

Johnny Sain is the one who put the title "pitching coach" on the map. When I was pitching in the minors, I didn't even have a pitching coach; the manager did everything. Wherever Sain went, pitching staffs did extremely well. Now, what does that tell you? There were pitchers who won 20 games for him who had never done it before and never did it again without him.

So to meet him and then listen to him speak about his teachings and his philosophies are the richest gifts I've ever had. He allowed me to really understand why he was able to get out of pitchers what a lot of other people couldn't.

From my selfish point of view, my reason for picking his brain was to help myself grow as a pitching coach. He had so much to offer. With his track record and the reputation, I would have been a damned fool *not* to pick his brain.

Johnny Sain coached a 20-game winner 16 times with nine different pitchers. Come on, nobody's going to get close to that anymore because the four-man rotation is history. In Atlanta, Glavine won 20 five times. Maddux just once; four times he won 19. Denny Neagle, once. John Smoltz, once. So, for me, there are eight 20-game winners and four different pitchers.

I brought Johnny out to Wrigley Field five or six years ago because he lives outside Chicago. He watched Maddux and Glavine throw. First thing he said was, "Hey, man, Maddux has got some kind of good movement on that ball." And then he watched Tommy, and said, "I love to watch him pitch because he dangles the ball out there and then pulls the string on it." He didn't want to come out to the park because he thought he was interfering. Can you imagine that?

I'm carrying on his torch. He knows it, and I know it. He still sends me some of his memorabilia, just so I can keep some of the stuff he's told me about. He sent me an audio tape of the game in the World Series when he beat Bob Feller 1-0.

He always closes his letters, "To the second best pitching coach in the game . . . from the first." That's his way of reminding me: *I did a lot more than you did.*

And you know what? I don't mind that a bit.

LEO MAZZONE'S
PLAYING CAREER

Year	Club	W-L	ERA	G	GS	CG	SHO	SV	IP	H	R	ER	BB	SO
1967	Medford	6-6	3.45	22	13	1	1	—	94	103	51	36	36	94
1968	Decatur	0-1	9.00	5	0	0	0	—	7	12	7	7	1	8
	Medford	5-5	4.97	29	8	0	0	—	76	78	49	42	34	91
1969	Decatur	15-10	2.52	26	26	17	4	0	186	177	79	52	58	151
1970	Amarillo	0-0	4.50	9	0	0	0	0	14	15	7	7	4	11*
1971	Amarillo	2-3	3.55	32	2	0	0	5	66	64	30	26	28	45
1972	Amarillo	9-8	2.26	29	13	6	3	1	136	129	46	34	38	119
1973	Amarillo	5-5	5.48	29	8	0	0	0	93	128	71	57	32	63
1974	Monterrey	3-6	5.42	16	12	2	0	1	73	85	49	44	30	44
	Birm.	4-6	4.29	30	6	2	0	4	84	92	45	40	36	45
1975	Birm.	0-1	3.75	8	0	0	0	1	12	9	5	5	6	5
	Tuscon	4-5	4.18	39	0	0	0	4	56	64	29	26	32	38
TOTALS		53-56	3.77	274	88	28	8	16	897	956	468	376	335	714

FOR THE RECORD

Over 100 pitchers have passed through Atlanta during the tenure of manager Bobby Cox and pitching coach Leo Mazzone. One, John Smoltz, has been there for the duration. Others lasted months, weeks and even days. Pity poor Joe Winkelsas, whose major-league record consists of one appearance in 1999 that lasted for a third of an inning. He gave up four hits and two runs. His major-league earned run average, based on that lone appearance, is 54.00.

At least two pitchers there for most of the run—Greg Maddux and Tom Glavine—will someday be enshrined in the Hall of Fame. A third, John Smoltz, also has a chance.

It is instructive to look at the records and compare what pitchers have done when in a Braves uniform as opposed to what they did before and after. One web site specializing in sabermetrics did a statistical comparison of the careers of pitchers when they were in Atlanta and when they played elsewhere.

Coached by Mazzone:
3.38 ERA / 6.9 SO per 9 innings / 3 BB per nine innings / 0.7 HR per 9 innings.

When not coached by Mazzone:
4.17 ERA / 5.9 SO per 9 innings / 3.3 BB per nine innings / 0.9 HR per 9 innings

As Leo likes to say, that's a pretty good track record.

Here are the records of notable pitchers who thrived under the tutelage of Leo Mazzone:

STEVE AVERY

Year	Age	Tm	Lg	W	L	G	GS	CG	SHO	SV	IP	H	ER	HR	BB	SO	ERA
1990	20	ATL	NL	3	11	21	20	1	1	0	99.0	121	62	7	45	75	5.64
1991	21	ATL	NL	18	8	35	35	3	1	0	210.3	189	79	21	65	137	3.38
1992	22	ATL	NL	11	11	35	35	2	2	0	233.7	216	83	14	71	129	3.20
1993	23	ATL	NL	18	6	35	35	3	1	0	223.3	216	73	14	43	125	2.94
1994	24	ATL	NL	8	3	24	24	1	0	0	151.7	127	68	15	55	122	4.04
1995	25	ATL	NL	7	13	29	29	3	1	0	173.3	165	90	22	52	141	4.67
1996	26	ATL	NL	7	10	24	23	1	0	0	131.0	146	65	10	40	86	4.47
1997	27	BOS	AL	6	7	22	18	0	0	0	96.7	127	69	15	49	51	6.42
1998	28	BOS	AL	10	7	34	23	0	0	0	123.7	128	69	14	64	57	5.02
1999	29	CIN	NL	6	7	19	19	0	0	0	96.0	75	55	11	78	51	5.16
10 Yr WL%	.531			94	83	278	261	14	6	0	1538.7	1510	713	143	562	974	4.17
162 Game Avg				11	10	35	32	1	0	0	194.1	190	89	18	70	122	4.17
Career High				18	13	35	35	3	2	0	233.7	216	90	22	78	141	2.94

JOHN BURKETT

Year	Age	Tm	Lg	W	L	G	GS	CG	SHO	SV	IP	H	ER	HR	BB	SO	ERA
1987	22	SFG	NL	0	0	3	0	0	0	0	6.0	7	3	2	3	5	4.50
1990	25	SFG	NL	14	7	33	32	2	0	1	204.0	201	86	18	61	118	3.79
1991	26	SFG	NL	12	11	36	34	3	1	0	206.7	223	96	19	60	131	4.18
1992	27	SFG	NL	13	9	32	32	3	1	0	189.7	194	81	13	45	107	3.84
1993	28	SFG	NL	22	7	34	34	2	1	0	231.7	224	94	18	40	145	3.65
1994	29	SFG	NL	6	8	25	25	0	0	0	159.3	176	64	14	36	85	3.62
1995	30	FLA	NL	14	14	30	30	4	0	0	188.3	208	90	22	57	126	4.30
1996	31	FLA	NL	6	10	24	24	1	0	0	154.0	154	74	15	42	108	4.32
		TEX	AL	5	2	10	10	1	1	0	68.7	75	31	4	16	47	4.06
		TOT		11	12	34	34	2	1	0	222.7	229	105	19	58	155	4.24
1997	32	TEX	AL	9	12	30	30	2	0	0	189.3	240	96	20	30	139	4.56
1998	33	TEX	AL	9	13	32	32	0	0	0	195.0	230	123	19	46	131	5.68
1999	34	TEX	AL	9	8	30	25	0	0	0	147.3	184	92	18	46	96	5.62
2000	35	ATL	NL	10	6	31	22	0	0	0	134.3	162	73	13	51	110	4.89
2001	36	ATL	NL	12	12	34	34	1	1	0	219.3	187	74	17	70	187	3.04
2002	37	BOS	AL	13	8	29	29	1	1	0	173.0	199	87	25	50	124	4.53
14 Yr WL%	.548			154	127	413	393	20	6	1	2466.7	2664	1164	237	653	1659	4.25
162 Game Avg				12	10	34	33	1	0	0	208.1	224	98	19	55	139	4.25
Career High				22	14	36	34	4	1	1	231.7	240	123	25	70	187	3.04

IN 1991 AT THE AGE OF 21, AVERY WAS THE NLCS MOST
VALUABLE PLAYER AFTER BEATING THE PIRATES TWICE IN
1-0 GAMES.

TOM GLAVINE

Year	Age	Tm	Lg	W	L	G	GS	CG	SHO	SV	IP	H	ER	HR	BB	SO	ERA
1987	21	ATL	NL	2	4	9	9	0	0	0	50.3	55	31	5	33	20	5.54
1988	22	ATL	NL	7	17	34	34	1	0	0	195.3	201	99	12	63	84	4.56
1989	23	ATL	NL	14	8	29	29	6	4	0	186.0	172	76	20	40	90	3.68
1990	24	ATL	NL	10	12	33	33	1	0	0	214.3	232	102	18	78	129	4.28
1991	25	ATL	NL	20	11	34	34	9	1	0	246.7	201	70	17	69	192	2.55
1992	26	ATL	NL	20	8	33	33	7	5	0	225.0	197	69	6	70	129	2.76
1993	27	ATL	NL	22	6	36	36	4	2	0	239.3	236	85	16	90	120	3.20
1994	28	ATL	NL	13	9	25	25	2	0	0	165.3	173	73	10	70	140	3.97
1995	29	ATL	NL	16	7	29	29	3	1	0	198.7	182	68	9	66	127	3.08
1996	30	ATL	NL	15	10	36	36	1	0	0	235.3	222	78	14	85	181	2.98
1997	31	ATL	NL	14	7	33	33	5	2	0	240.0	197	79	20	79	152	2.96
1998	32	ATL	NL	20	6	33	33	4	3	0	229.3	202	63	13	74	157	2.47
1999	33	ATL	NL	14	11	35	35	2	0	0	234.0	259	107	18	83	138	4.12
2000	34	ATL	NL	21	9	35	35	4	2	0	241.0	222	91	24	65	152	3.40
2001	35	ATL	NL	16	7	35	35	1	1	0	219.3	213	87	24	97	116	3.57
2002	36	ATL	NL	18	11	36	36	2	1	0	224.7	210	74	21	78	127	2.96
16 Yr WL% .629				242	143	505	505	52	22	0	3344.7	3174	1252	247	1140	2054	3.37
162 Game Avg				16	9	34	34	3	1	0	225.2	213	84	16	76	138	3.37
Career High				22	17	36	36	9	5	0	246.7	259	107	24	97	192	2.47

CHARLIE LEIBRANDT

Year	Age	Tm	Lg	W	L	G	GS	CG	SHO	SV	IP	H	ER	HR	BB	SO	ERA*
1979	22	CIN	NL	0	0	3	0	0	0	0	4.3	2	0	0	2	1	0.
1980	23	CIN	NL	10	9	36	27	5	2	0	173.7	200	82	15	54	62	4.25
1981	24	CIN	NL	1	1	7	4	1	1	0	30.0	28	12	0	15	9	3.60
1982	25	CIN	NL	5	7	36	11	0	0	2	107.7	130	61	4	48	34	5.10
1984	27	KCR	AL	11	7	23	23	0	0	0	143.7	158	58	11	38	53	3.63
1985	28	KCR	AL	17	9	33	33	8	3	0	237.7	223	71	17	68	108	2.69
1986	29	KCR	AL	14	11	35	34	8	1	0	231.3	238	105	18	63	108	4.09
1987	30	KCR	AL	16	11	35	35	8	3	0	240.3	235	91	23	74	151	3.41
1988	31	KCR	AL	13	12	35	35	7	2	0	243.0	244	86	20	62	125	3.19
1989	32	KCR	AL	5	11	33	27	3	1	0	161.0	196	92	13	54	73	5.14
1990	33	ATL	NL	9	11	24	24	5	2	0	162.3	164	57	9	35	76	3.16
1991	34	ATL	NL	15	13	36	36	1	1	0	229.7	212	89	18	56	128	3.49
1992	35	ATL	NL	15	7	32	31	5	2	0	193.0	191	72	9	42	104	3.36
1993	36	TEX	AL	9	10	26	26	1	0	0	150.3	169	76	15	45	89	4.55
14 Yr WL% .541				140	119	394	346	52	18	2	2308.0	2390	952	172	656	1121	3.71
162 Game Avg				12	10	36	31	4	1	0	212.1	219	87	15	60	103	3.71
Career High				17	13	36	36	8	3	2	243.0	244	105	23	74	151	2.69

KERRY LIGTENBERG

Year	Age	Tm	Lg	W	L	G	GS	CG	SHO	SV	IP	H	ER	HR	BB	SO	ERA
1997	26	ATL	NL	1	0	15	0	0	0	1	15.0	12	5	4	4	19	3.00
1998	27	ATL	NL	3	2	75	0	0	0	30	73.0	51	22	6	24	79	2.71
2000	29	ATL	NL	2	3	59	0	0	0	12	52.3	43	21	7	24	51	3.61
2001	30	ATL	NL	3	3	53	0	0	0	1	59.7	50	20	4	30	56	3.02
2002	31	ATL	NL	3	4	52	0	0	0	0	66.7	52	22	6	33	51	2.97
5 Yr WL% .500				12	12	254	0	0	0	44	266.7	208	90	27	115	256	3.04
162 Game Avg				3	3	68	0	0	0	11	71.4	55	24	7	30	68	3.04
Career High				3	4	75	0	0	0	30	73.0	52	22	7	33	79	2.71

GREG MADDUX

Year	Age	Tm	Lg	W	L	G	GS	CG	SHO	SV	IP	H	ER	HR	BB	SO	ERA
1986	20	CHC	NL	2	4	6	5	1	0	0	31.0	44	19	3	11	20	5.52
1987	21	CHC	NL	6	14	30	27	1	1	0	155.7	181	97	17	74	101	5.61
1988	22	CHC	NL	18	8	34	34	9	3	0	249.0	230	88	13	81	140	3.18
1989	23	CHC	NL	19	12	35	35	7	1	0	238.3	222	78	13	82	135	2.95
1990	24	CHC	NL	15	15	35	35	8	2	0	237.0	242	91	11	71	144	3.46
1991	25	CHC	NL	15	11	37	37	7	2	0	263.0	232	98	18	66	198	3.35
1992	26	CHC	NL	20	11	35	35	9	4	0	268.0	201	65	7	70	199	2.18
1993	27	ATL	NL	20	10	36	36	8	1	0	267.0	228	70	14	52	197	2.36
1994	28	ATL	NL	16	6	25	25	10	3	0	202.0	150	35	4	31	156	1.56
1995	29	ATL	NL	19	2	28	28	10	3	0	209.7	147	38	8	23	181	1.63
1996	30	ATL	NL	15	11	35	35	5	1	0	245.0	225	74	11	28	172	2.72
1997	31	ATL	NL	19	4	33	33	5	2	0	232.7	200	57	9	20	177	2.20
1998	32	ATL	NL	18	9	34	34	9	5	0	251.0	201	62	13	45	204	2.22
1999	33	ATL	NL	19	9	33	33	4	0	0	219.3	258	87	16	37	136	3.57
2000	34	ATL	NL	19	9	35	35	6	3	0	249.3	225	83	19	42	190	3.00
2001	35	ATL	NL	17	11	34	34	3	3	0	233.0	220	79	20	27	173	3.05
2002	36	ATL	NL	16	6	34	34	0	0	0	199.3	194	58	14	45	118	2.62
17 Yr WL% .642				273	152	539	535	102	34	0	3750.3	3400	1179	210	805	2641	2.83
162 Game Avg				17	9	34	33	6	2	0	237.4	215	74	13	50	167	2.83
Career High				20	15	37	37	10	5	0	268.0	258	98	20	82	204	1.56

MAZZONE WITH MADDUX IN THE BULLPEN AT WRIGLEY FIELD.

GREG MCMICHAEL

Year	Age	Tm	Lg	W	L	G	GS	CG	SHO	SV	IP	H	ER	HR	BB	SO	ERA
1993	26	ATL	NL	2	3	74	0	0	0	19	91.7	68	21	3	29	89	2.06
1994	27	ATL	NL	4	6	51	0	0	0	21	58.7	66	25	1	19	47	3.84
1995	28	ATL	NL	7	2	67	0	0	0	2	80.7	64	25	8	32	74	2.79
1996	29	ATL	NL	5	3	73	0	0	0	2	86.7	84	31	4	27	78	3.22
1997	30	NYM	NL	7	10	73	0	0	0	7	87.7	73	29	8	27	81	2.98
1998	31	NYM	NL	1	2	22	0	0	0	0	22.3	23	10	1	14	22	4.03
		LAD	NL	0	1	12	0	0	0	1	14.3	17	7	1	6	11	4.40
		NYM	NL	4	1	30	0	0	0	1	31.0	41	14	7	15	22	4.06
		TOT	NL	5	4	64	0	0	0	2	67.7	81	31	9	35	55	4.12
1999	32	NYM	NL	1	1	19	0	0	0	0	18.7	20	10	3	8	18	4.82
		OAK	AL	0	0	17	0	0	0	0	15.0	15	9	3	12	3	5.40
		TOT	NL	1	1	36	0	0	0	0	33.7	35	19	6	20	21	5.08
2000	33	ATL	NL	0	0	15	0	0	0	0	16.3	12	8	3	4	14	4.41
8Yr WL% .517				31	29	453	0	0	0	53	523.0	483	189	42	193	459	3.25
162 Game Avg				4	4	68	0	0	0	7	78.5	72	28	6	28	68	3.25
Career High				7	10	74	0	0	0	21	91.7	84	31	9	35	89	2.06

KENT MERCKER

Year	Age	Tm	Lg	W	L	G	GS	CG	SHO	SV	IP	H	ER	HR	BB	SO	ERA
1989	21	ATL	NL	0	0	2	1	0	0	0	4.3	8	6	0	6	4	12.46
1990	22	ATL	NL	4	7	36	0	0	0	7	48.3	43	17	6	24	39	3.17
1991	23	ATL	NL	5	3	50	4	0	0	6	73.3	56	21	5	35	62	2.58
1992	24	ATL	NL	3	2	53	0	0	0	6	68.3	51	26	4	35	49	3.42
1993	25	ATL	NL	3	1	43	6	0	0	0	66.0	52	21	2	36	59	2.86
1994	26	ATL	NL	9	4	20	17	2	1	0	112.3	90	43	16	45	111	3.45
1995	27	ATL	NL	7	8	29	26	0	0	0	143.0	140	66	16	61	102	4.15
1996	28	BAL	AL	3	6	14	12	0	0	0	58.0	73	50	12	35	22	7.76
		CLE	AL	1	0	10	0	0	0	0	11.7	10	4	1	3	7	3.09
		TOT	AL	4	6	24	12	0	0	0	69.7	83	54	13	38	29	6.98
1997	29	CIN	NL	8	11	28	25	0	0	0	144.7	135	63	16	62	75	3.92
1998	30	STL	NL	11	11	30	29	0	0	0	161.7	199	91	11	53	72	5.07
1999	31	STL	NL	6	5	25	18	0	0	0	103.7	125	59	16	51	64	5.12
		BOS	AL	2	0	5	5	0	0	0	25.7	23	10	0	13	17	3.51
		TOT		8	5	30	23	0	0	0	129.3	148	69	16	64	81	4.80
2000	32	ANA	AL	1	3	21	7	0	0	0	48.3	57	35	12	29	30	6.52
2002	34	COL	NL	3	1	58	0	0	0	0	44.0	55	30	12	22	37	6.14
13 Yr WL% .516				66	62	424	150	2	1	191	113.3	1117	542	129	510	750	4.38
162 Game Avg				7	7	50	17	0	0	2	131.9	132	64	15	60	88	4.38
Career High				11	11	58	29	2	1	7	161.7	199	91	16	64	111	2.58

KEVIN MILLWOOD

Year	Age	Tm	Lg	W	L	G	GS	CG	SHO	SV	IP	H	ER	HR	BB	SO	ERA
1997	22	ATL	NL	5	3	12	8	0	0	0	51.3	55	23	1	21	42	4.03
1998	23	ATL	NL	17	8	31	29	3	1	0	174.3	175	79	18	56	163	4.08
1999	24	ATL	NL	18	7	33	33	2	0	0	228.0	168	68	24	59	205	2.68
2000	25	ATL	NL	10	13	36	35	0	0	0	212.7	213	110	26	62	168	4.66
2001	26	ATL	NL	7	7	21	21	0	0	0	121.0	121	58	20	40	84	4.31
2002	27	ATL	NL	18	8	35	34	1	1	0	217.0	186	78	16	65	178	3.24
6 Yr WL% .620				75	46	168	160	6	2	0	1004.3	918	416	105	303	840	3.73
162 Game Avg				15	9	34	33	1	0	0	208.2	190	86	21	62	174	3.73
Career High				18	13	36	35	3	1	0	228.0	213	110	26	65	205	2.68

DENNY NEAGLE

Year	Age	Tm	Lg	W	L	G	GS	CG	SHO	SV	IP	H	ER	HR	BB	SO	ERA
1991	22	MIN	AL	0	1	7	3	0	0	0	20.0	28	9	3	7	14	4.05
1992	23	PIT	NL	4	6	55	6	0	0	2	86.3	81	43	9	43	77	4.48
1993	24	PIT	NL	3	5	50	7	0	0	1	81.3	82	48	10	37	73	5.31
1994	25	PIT	NL	9	10	24	24	2	0	0	137.0	135	78	18	49	122	5.12
1995	26	PIT	NL	13	8	31	31	5	1	0	209.7	221	80	20	45	150	3.43
1996	27	PIT	NL	14	6	27	27	1	0	0	182.7	186	62	21	34	131	3.05
		ATL	NL	2	3	6	6	1	0	0	38.7	40	24	5	14	18	5.59
		TOT	NL	16	9	33	33	2	0	0	221.3	226	86	26	48	149	3.50
1997	28	ATL	NL	20	5	34	34	4	4	0	233.3	204	77	18	49	172	2.97
1998	29	ATL	NL	16	11	32	31	5	2	0	210.3	196	83	25	60	165	3.55
1999	30	CIN	NL	9	5	20	19	0	0	0	111.7	95	53	23	40	76	4.27
2000	31	CIN	NL	8	2	18	18	0	0	0	117.7	111	46	15	50	88	3.52
		NYY	AL	7	7	16	15	1	0	0	91.3	99	59	16	31	58	5.81
		TOT		15	9	34	33	1	0	0	209.0	210	105	31	81	146	4.52
2001	32	COL	NL	9	8	30	30	0	0	0	170.7	192	102	29	60	139	5.38
2002	33	COL	NL	8	11	35	28	1	0	0	164.3	170	96	26	63	111	5.26
12 Yr WL% .581				122	88	385	279	20	7	3	1855.0	1840	860	238	582	1394	4.17
162 Game Avg				12	9	39	28	2	0	0	190.0	188	88	24	59	142	4.17
Career High				20	11	55	34	5	4	2	233.3	226	105	31	81	172	2.97

DENNY NEAGLE THROWS A CHANGE-UP. HE WON 20 GAMES IN 1997 BEFORE HE HURT HIS SHOULDER.

ALEJANDRO PEÑA

Year	Age	Tm	Lg	W	L	G	GS	CG	SHO	SV	IP	H	ER	HR	BB	SO	ERA
1981	22	LAD	NL	1	1	14	0	0	0	2	25.3	18	8	2	11	14	2.84
1982	23	LAD	NL	0	2	29	0	0	0	0	35.7	37	19	2	21	20	4.79
1983	24	LAD	NL	12	9	34	26	4	3	1	177.0	152	54	7	51	120	2.75
1984	25	LAD	NL	12	6	28	28	8	4	0	199.3	186	55	7	46	135	2.48
1985	26	LAD	NL	0	1	2	1	0	0	0	4.3	7	4	1	3	2	8.31
1986	27	LAD	NL	1	2	24	10	0	0	1	70.0	74	38	6	30	46	4.89
1987	28	LAD	NL	2	7	37	7	0	0	11	87.3	82	34	9	37	76	3.50
1988	29	LAD	NL	6	7	60	0	0	0	12	94.3	75	20	4	27	83	1.91
1989	30	LAD	NL	4	3	53	0	0	0	5	76.0	62	18	6	18	75	2.13
1990	31	NYM	NL	3	3	52	0	0	0	5	76.0	71	27	4	22	76	3.20
1991	32	NYM	NL	6	1	44	0	0	0	4	63.0	63	19	5	19	49	2.71
		ATL	NL	2	0	15	0	0	0	11	19.3	11	3	1	3	13	1.40
		TOT	NL	8	1	59	0	0	0	15	82.3	74	22	6	22	62	2.40
1992	33	ATL	NL	1	6	41	0	0	0	15	42.0	40	19	7	13	34	4.07
1994	35	PIT	NL	3	2	22	0	0	0	7	28.7	22	16	4	10	27	5.02
1995	36	BOS	AL	1	1	17	0	0	0	0	24.3	33	20	5	12	25	7.40
		FLA	NL	2	0	13	0	0	0	0	18.0	11	3	2	3	21	1.50
		ATL	NL	0	0	14	0	0	0	0	13.0	11	6	1	4	18	4.15
		TOT	NL	2	0	27	0	0	0	0	31.0	22	9	3	7	39	2.61
		TOT		3	1	44	0	0	0	0	55.3	55	29	8	19	64	4.72
1996	37	FLA	NL	0	1	4	0	0	0	0	4.0	4	2	2	1	5	4.50
15 Yr WL% .519				56	52	503	72	12	7	74	1057.7	959	365	75	331	839	3.11
162 Game Avg				6	6	59	8	1	0	8	125.1	113	43	8	39	99	3.11
Career High				12	9	60	28	8	4	15	199.3	186	55	9	51	135	1.91

MIKE REMLINGER

Year	Age	Tm	Lg	W	L	G	GS	CG	SHO	SV	IP	H	ER	HR	BB	SO	ERA
1991	25	SFG	NL	2	1	8	6	1	1	0	35.0	36	17	5	20	19	4.37
1994	28	NYM	NL	1	5	10	9	0	0	0	54.7	55	28	9	35	33	4.61
1995	29	NYM	NL	0	1	5	0	0	0	0	5.7	7	4	1	2	6	6.35
		CIN	NL	0	0	2	0	0	0	0	1.0	2	1	0	3	1	9.00
		TOT	NL	0	1	7	0	0	0	0	6.7	9	5	1	5	7	6.75
1996	30	CIN	NL	0	1	19	4	0	0	0	27.3	24	17	4	19	19	5.60
1997	31	CIN	NL	8	8	69	12	2	0	2	124.0	100	57	11	60	145	4.14
1998	32	CIN	NL	8	15	35	28	1	1	0	164.3	164	88	23	87	144	4.82
1999	33	ATL	NL	10	1	73	0	0	0	1	83.7	66	22	9	35	81	2.37
2000	34	ATL	NL	5	3	71	0	0	0	12	72.7	55	28	6	37	72	3.47
2001	35	ATL	NL	3	3	74	0	0	0	1	75.0	67	23	9	23	93	2.76
2002	36	ATL	NL	7	3	73	0	0	0	0	68.0	48	15	3	28	69	1.99
10 Yr WL% .518				44	41	439	59	4	2	16	711.3	624	300	80	349	682	3.80
162 Game Avg				6	5	59	8	0	0	2	97.1	85	40	10	47	93	3.80
Career High				10	15	74	28	2	1	12	164.3	164	88	23	87	145	1.99

JOHN ROCKER

Year	Age	Tm	Lg	W	L	G	GS	CG	SHO	SV	IP	H	ER	HR	BB	SO	ERA
1998	23	ATL	NL	1	3	47	0	0	0	2	38.0	22	9	4	22	42	2.13
1999	24	ATL	NL	4	5	74	0	0	0	38	72.3	47	20	5	37	104	2.49
2000	25	ATL	NL	1	2	59	0	0	0	24	53.0	42	17	5	48	77	2.89
2001	26	ATL	NL	2	2	30	0	0	0	19	32.0	25	11	2	16	36	3.09
		CLE	AL	3	7	38	0	0	0	4	34.7	33	21	2	25	43	5.45
		TOT		5	9	68	0	0	0	23	66.7	58	32	4	41	79	4.32
2002	27	TEX	AL	2	3	30	0	0	0	1	24.3	29	18	5	13	30	6.66
5 Yr WL% .371				13	22	278	0	0	0	88	254.3	198	96	23	161	332	3.40
162 Game Avg				3	5	68	0	0	0	21	62.2	48	23	5	39	81	3.40
Career High				5	9	74	0	0	0	38	72.3	58	32	5	48	104	2.49

RUDY SEANEZ

Year	Age	Tm	Lg	W	L	G	GS	CG	SHO	SV	IP	H	ER	HR	BB	SO	ERA
1989	20	CLE	AL	0	0	5	0	0	0	0	5.0	1	2	0	4	7	3.60
1990	21	CLE	AL	2	1	24	0	0	0	0	27.3	22	17	2	25	24	5.60
1991	22	CLE	AL	0	0	5	0	0	0	0	5.0	10	9	2	7	7	16.20
1993	24	SDP	NL	0	0	3	0	0	0	0	3.3	8	5	1	2	1	13.50
1994	25	LAD	NL	1	1	17	0	0	0	0	23.7	24	7	2	9	18	2.66
1995	26	LAD	NL	1	3	37	0	0	0	3	34.7	39	26	5	18	29	6.75
1998	29	ATL	NL	4	1	34	0	0	0	2	36.0	25	11	2	16	50	2.75
1999	30	ATL	NL	6	1	56	0	0	0	3	53.7	47	20	3	21	41	3.35
2000	31	ATL	NL	2	4	23	0	0	0	2	21.0	15	10	3	9	20	4.29
2001	32	SDP	NL	0	2	26	0	0	0	1	24.0	15	7	3	15	24	2.62
		ATL	NL	0	0	12	0	0	0	0	12.0	8	4	1	4	17	3.00
		TOT	NL	0	2	38	0	0	0	1	36.0	23	11	4	19	41	2.75
2002	33	TEX	AL	1	3	33	0	0	0	0	33.0	28	21	5	24	40	5.73
11 Yr WL% .515				17	16	275	0	0	0	11	278.7	242	139	29	154	278	4.49
162 Game Avg				4	3	68	0	0	0	2	68.9	59	34	7	38	68	4.49
Career High				6	1	56	0	0	0	3	53.7	47	20	3	21	41	3.35

JOHN SMOLTZ

Year	Ag	Tm	Lg	W	L	G	GS	CG	SHO	SV	IP	H	ER	HR	BB	SO	ERA
1988	21	ATL	NL	2	7	12	12	0	0	0	64.0	74	39	10	33	37	5.48
1989	22	ATL	NL	12	11	29	29	5	0	0	208.0	160	68	15	72	168	2.94
1990	23	ATL	NL	14	11	34	34	6	2	0	231.3	206	99	20	90	170	3.85
1991	24	ATL	NL	14	13	36	36	5	0	0	229.7	206	97	16	77	148	3.80
1992	25	ATL	NL	15	12	35	35	9	3	0	246.7	206	78	17	80	215	2.85
1993	26	ATL	NL	15	11	35	35	3	1	0	243.7	208	98	23	100	208	3.62
1994	27	ATL	NL	6	10	21	21	1	0	0	134.7	120	62	15	48	113	4.14
1995	28	ATL	NL	12	7	29	29	2	1	0	192.7	166	68	15	72	193	3.18
1996	29	ATL	NL	24	8	35	35	6	2	0	253.7	199	83	19	55	276	2.94
1997	30	ATL	NL	15	12	35	35	7	2	0	256.0	234	86	21	63	241	3.02
1998	31	ATL	NL	17	3	26	26	2	2	0	167.7	145	54	10	44	173	2.90
1999	32	ATL	NL	11	8	29	29	1	1	0	186.3	168	66	14	40	156	3.19
2001	34	ATL	NL	3	3	36	5	0	0	10	59.0	53	22	7	10	57	3.36
2002	35	ATL	NL	3	2	75	0	0	0	55	80.3	59	29	4	24	85	3.25
14 Yr WL% .580				163	118	467	361	47	14	65	2553.7	2204	949	206	808	2240	3.34
162 Game Avg				13	9	38	29	3	1	5	209.7	181	77	16	66	183	3.34
Career High				24	13	75	36	9	3	55	256.0	234	99	23	100	276	2.85

MAZZONE WALKS IN FROM A SIDE SESSION WITH SMOLTZ.

MIKE STANTON

Year	Age	Tm	Lg	W	L	G	GS	CG	SHO	SV	IP	H	ER	HR	BB	SO	ERA
1989	22	ATL	NL	0	1	20	0	0	0	7	24.0	17	4	0	8	27	1.50
1990	23	ATL	NL	0	3	7	0	0	0	2	7.0	16	14	1	4	7	18.00
1991	24	ATL	NL	5	5	74	0	0	0	7	78.0	62	25	6	21	54	2.88
1992	25	ATL	NL	5	4	65	0	0	0	8	63.7	59	29	6	20	44	4.10
1993	26	ATL	NL	4	6	63	0	0	0	27	52.0	51	27	4	29	43	4.67
1994	27	ATL	NL	3	1	49	0	0	0	3	45.7	41	18	2	26	35	3.55
1995	28	ATL	NL	1	1	26	0	0	0	1	19.3	31	12	3	6	13	5.59
		BOS	AL	1	0	22	0	0	0	0	21.0	17	7	3	8	10	3.00
		TOT		2	1	48	0	0	0	1	40.3	48	19	6	14	23	4.24
1996	29	BOS	AL	4	3	59	0	0	0	1	56.3	58	24	9	23	46	3.83
		TEX	AL	0	1	22	0	0	0	0	22.3	20	8	2	4	14	3.22
		TOTAL		4	4	81	0	0	0	1	78.7	78	32	11	27	60	3.66
1997	30	NYY	AL	6	1	64	0	0	0	3	66.7	50	19	3	34	70	2.56
1998	31	NYY	AL	4	1	67	0	0	0	6	79.0	71	48	13	26	69	5.47
1999	32	NYY	AL	2	2	73	1	0	0	0	62.3	71	30	5	18	59	4.33
2000	33	NYY	AL	2	3	69	0	0	0	0	68.0	68	31	5	24	75	4.10
2001	34	NYY	AL	9	4	76	0	0	0	0	80.3	80	23	4	29	78	2.58
2002	35	NYY	AL	7	1	79	0	0	0	6	78.0	73	26	4	28	44	3.00
14 Yr WL% .589				53	37	835	1	0	0	71	823.7	785	345	70	308	688	3.77
162 Game Avg				4	3	67	0	0	0	5	67.0	63	28	5	25	55	3.77
Career High				9	6	81	1	0	0	27	80.3	80	48	13	34	78	2.56

MARK WOHLERS

Year	Age	Tm	Lg	W	L	G	GS	CG	SHO	SV	IP	H	ER	HR	BB	SO	ERA
1991	21	ATL	NL	3	1	17	0	0	0	2	19.7	17	7	1	13	13	3.20
1992	22	ATL	NL	1	2	32	0	0	0	4	35.3	28	10	0	14	17	2.55
1993	23	ATL	NL	6	2	46	0	0	0	0	48.0	37	24	2	22	45	4.50
1994	24	ATL	NL	7	2	51	0	0	0	1	51.0	51	26	1	33	58	4.59
1995	25	ATL	NL	7	3	65	0	0	0	25	64.7	51	15	2	24	90	2.09
1996	26	ATL	NL	2	4	77	0	0	0	39	77.3	71	26	8	21	100	3.03
1997	27	ATL	NL	5	7	71	0	0	0	33	69.3	57	27	4	38	92	3.50
1998	28	ATL	NL	0	1	27	0	0	0	8	20.3	18	23	2	33	22	10.18
1999	29	ATL	NL	0	0	2	0	0	0	0	0.7	1	2	0	6	0	27.00
2000	30	CIN	NL	1	2	20	0	0	0	0	28.0	19	14	3	17	20	4.50
2001	31	CIN	NL	3	1	30	0	0	0	0	32.0	36	14	5	7	21	3.94
		NYY	AL	1	0	31	0	0	0	0	35.7	33	18	3	18	33	4.54
		TOT		4	1	61	0	0	0	0	67.7	69	32	8	25	54	4.26
2002	32	CLE	AL	3	4	64	0	0	0	7	71.3	71	38	6	26	46	4.79
12 Years				39	29	533	0	0	0	119	553.3	490	244	37	272	557	3.97
162 Game Avg				4	3	68	0	0	0	15	70.6	62	31	4	34	71	3.97
Career High				7	7	77	0	0	0	39	77.3	71	38	8	38	100	2.09

Acknowledgments

FROM LEO MAZZONE:

I want to thank my mom and dad, Maxine and Tony Mazzone, for their love and support. My dad was my manager and coach in the Little League, Pony League, American Legion, at St. Peter's Catholic High School, the Pen Mar League and the Twilight League.

Also, thanks to Junie Perry, the player/manager for the Keyser, West Virginia Pen Mar League and scout for the San Francisco Giants. And to Frank Patrone, my coach in the Pen Mar and Twilight Leagues, and at St. Peter's Catholic High School. Also to Bill Angle, coach at St. Peter's, and Nick Perlozo, the manager of the American Legion team in Cumberland, Maryland. And Luther Clay, who was an umpire from Piedmont, West Virginia and gave me the corners, big time. And to all the nuns and priests at St. Peter's Archdiocese.

Professionally, I'd like to thank all the great pitchers I've had the privilege of coaching. And special thanks to Bobby Cox, Jim Beauchamp, Bobby Dews and, of course, Johnny Sain.

Finally, thanks to my family. And to my marketing representative Todd Thrasher and the team at Leader Enterprises.

FROM SCOTT FREEMAN:

Thanks to Leo Mazzone for sharing his wonderful memories of the best decade of baseball in the history of Atlanta. I enjoyed watching it unfold as much as I enjoyed listening to the stories.

Thanks to Lee Walburn, editor emeritus of *Atlanta Magazine*; it was a feature story he assigned and edited that led me to interview Leo for the first time. Thanks also to Rebecca Poynor Burns, editor of *Atlanta Magazine*, and to Deborah Paul, executive vice president and editorial director of Emmis Publications, for their support. And thanks to all my friends and colleagues at *Atlanta Magazine*.

Thanks also to Anne Isenhower, Carrolle King and Chank Middleton, Ken and Alicia Lyon, William and Virginia Berry, Deb Miller, and Suzanne Espinosa, who shared the 1991 worst-to-first pennant race with me.

Thanks to my agents, David Black and Gary Morris, at the David Black Literary Agency in New York City. And to Gabe Rosen and all the folks at Sports Publishing L.L.C.

Also, to my family for their love and support through the years. And a special thanks to my dad, Wilson Freeman, who spent hours playing catch in our backyard as I struggled to learn how to pitch and took me to my first professional baseball game in 1966 at Atlanta-Fulton County Stadium. My talents as a pitcher were such that I decided I'd better learn how to write.